RENAMING ECSTASY

LATINO WRITINGS ON THE SACRED

Bilingual Press/Editorial Bilingüe

General Editor
  Gary D. Keller

Managing Editor
  Karen S. Van Hooft

Associate Editors
  Brian Ellis Cassity
  Cristina de Isasi
  Thea S. Kuticka
  Linda St. George Thurston

Editorial Board
  Juan Goytisolo
  Francisco Jiménez
  Mario Vargas Llosa

Address:
  Bilingual Press
  Hispanic Research Center
  Arizona State University
  P.O. Box 872702
  Tempe, Arizona 85287-2702
  (480) 965-3867

RENAMING ECSTASY

LATINO WRITINGS ON THE SACRED

Edited with an introduction by

Orlando Ricardo Menes

Bilingual Press/Editorial Bilingüe

Tempe, Arizona

ISBN 1-931010-15-3

Library of Congress Cataloging-in-Publication Data

Renaming ecstasy : Latino writings on the sacred / Orlando Ricardo Menes, editor.
    p. cm.
    ISBN 1-931010-15-3 (alk. paper)
    1. Religious poetry, American—History and criticism. 2. American poetry—Hispanic American authors—History and criticism. 3. Hispanic Americans—Religion. 4. Holy, The, in literature. I. Menes, Orlando Ricardo.

    PS310.R4 R46 2002
    811.009'382—dc21

                                                                  2002026163

PRINTED IN THE UNITED STATES OF AMERICA

Front cover art: Fides et Ratio *(1999) by Daniel Martín Díaz*

Cover and interior design by John Wincek, Aerocraft Charter Art Service

Acknowledgments

Partial funding provided by the Arizona Commission on the Arts through appropriations from the Arizona State Legislature and grants from the National Endowment for the Arts.

Permissions for use of the poems appear on pp. 155–57.

Contents

3   Shamans and *Babaláwos*

4   *Los Católicos:* Latino Catholics

5 Alternate Spiritualities:
Beauty and Nature as Realms of Sacredness

Appendix A

Appendix B

Introduction

Orlando Ricardo Menes

For years Latinos and Latinas have been writing poems rich in spirituality, yet this body of work has received scant attention by literary and cultural critics. In fact, most Americans know little about the spirituality of Latinos and if asked would almost certainly resort to stereotyped images drawn from television and the movies. These are too numerous to illustrate in detail but include the ever-present pious *abuelitas* (grandmothers) gathered around La Virgen de Guadalupe muttering prayers and holding dripping candles, Afro-Cuban hoodoo priests sacrificing goats and chickens to malevolent deities, blood-soaked penitents wearing crowns of thorns and dragging crosses during Good Friday processions, and the Mexican Day of the Dead complete with dancing skeletons, spooky skull masks, and fireworks. Of course, one would be right in saying that these simplistic images point to a general lack of understanding about Latinos, especially their diversity, which is why a particular focus on spirituality is important because it provides a window into a realm of identity that constitutes the very essence of a community's existence.

This anthology is the first of its kind to bring together a number of Latino/a poets, both emerging and established, who write of the sacred in ways that ultimately aim to redefine what constitutes our communion with the divine within the context of a multicultural America. Reflecting the multiple national origins of U.S. Latinos, the poetic voices here are compelling, textured, resonant. Together they sing as a polyphonous chorus to celebrate, question, and probe experiences of the sacred that defy those stereotypes all too common in popular culture.

For example, because of Latin America's mixture of cultures, traditional Catholicism exists alongside other spiritualities of African or indigenous origin. In their invocation of the divine, poets of Caribbean origin often draw inspiration from the myths and practices of Santería, a syncretic Afro-Cuban religion. Others write about topics that engage Latino Catholics: the lives of the saints, the nature of God, the sacraments, and other devotional practices that connect individuals to the community and give shape to their daily lives. A few Chicanas, here called Poets of Aztlán (the mythic Aztec homeland located in today's Southwest), even hybridize Christianity with the ancient religion of their indigenous ancestors, thereby establishing a continuum between the pre-Columbian past and the post-modern present. Still others divorce themselves from tradition, thereby discovering sacredness in art and nature.

Because this is a thematic collection, five categories have been created that take into account both poetics and spirituality. These are (1) Mestizo Sacredness: Poets of Aztlán; (2) Mestizo Sacredness: Poets of Caribbean Origin; (3) Shamans and *Babaláwos*; (4) *Los Católicos:* Latino Catholics; and (5) Alternate Spiritualities: Beauty and Nature as Realms of Sacredness. Of course, these categories are not absolute, and a few poets can easily be located in two or more, yet I hope that they serve the purpose of facilitating discussion.

Mestizo Sacredness: Poets of Aztlán

Proud of their mixed racial and cultural heritage, PAT MORA and NAOMI QUIÑONEZ have espoused a spiritual poetics of hybridity that gives voice to the dual consciousness of the mestiza, a theme that forms the basis of Gloria Anzaldúa's brilliant *Borderlands*/La Frontera: *The New Mestiza* (San Francisco: Aunt Lute Books, 1987; 2d ed., 1999). Because she is viewed as a synthesis of the Aztec and the Spanish, the Virgin of Guadalupe is the poets' particular focus. (For an in-depth discussion of this patron saint of Mexico and of cultural and religious *mestizaje* in general, please consult Appendix A.)

Of these two Chicana poets, it is PAT MORA in particular who has reenvisioned the figure of Our Lady of Guadalupe. For example, her poems "Consejos de Nuestra Señora" (Advice from Our Lady) and "Coatlicue's Rules" attempt to refashion Our Lady within a feminist ideology. In the former poem, for example, she is no longer the fragile and delicate girl commonly found in the ecclesial tradition. Instead, one finds a strong woman who is practical, intelligent, defiant, and self-sufficient. And quirky too. Without the intervention of the patriarchal church, she is able to talk directly to women, urging them to take control of their lives, their destinies. She tells them to "practice solitary levitation . . . [to] ignore [male-centered] halos. . . ." "Hijas," she exclaims to her daughters, "value contemplation." Mora empowers The Lady of Tepeyac to determine her own nature and existence in opposition to the male-centered mythologies of the Guadalupean tradition. "Holy men altered me," she says. "Alone, I write / my own legends."

Another poem of feminist advice is "Coatlicue's Rules." Here Our Lady of Guadalupe is identified with the Aztec goddess Coatlicue, "She of the Skirt with Serpents," mother of the sun, the moon, and the stars as well as all the other gods. Contrary to Christian iconography, the snake symbolized for the ancient Mexicans not Satan but rather perfection, immortality, wisdom, and peace. Unlike "Consejos de Nuestra Señora," this poem presents us with an image of Our Lady characterized more by irony than by reverence. Coatlicue, virgin-mother of 400 gods, appears uncertain about the child she carries in her womb, this sun god who also happens to be Christ. "You sense my ambivalence," Coatlicue says. "I'm blinded by his light." This reluctant mother also confronts the patriarchal power structure: "Men carved me, / wrote my story, and Eve's, Malinche's, Guadalupe's / Llorona's, snakes everywhere, even in our mouths." In one fell swoop Mora brilliantly combines in Coatlicue the three women who gave birth to modern Mexico: Eve, mother of all humanity in the Judeo-Christian tradition; Mary (Guadalupe), mother of Christ the Savior, mother of God himself; and La Malinche, interpreter and mistress to Hernán Cortés. Though much reviled in Mexican folklore for having aided the Spanish explorer in conquering the Aztecs, La Malinche more importantly represents the mother of *la raza*, the mixed-race Mexican people.

In "Litany to the Dark Goddess" one hears a rhapsodic voice, a priestess who sings the many names of the ancestral mother, whether she be Christian or Aztec, names that embody the multiple histories of Mexico. Here the worlds of myth and history, faith and blood coalesce to create beauty that is both primal and transcendent. The poet transforms herself into the priestess who chants herself into an ecstatic state where she, like the Dark Goddess, can become the "Dreamer of [her] Many Manifestations." Apart from the already mentioned Coatlicue, this syncretic litany (shifting from English to Spanish) catalogues many more maternal goddesses of the Aztec pantheon, including such curious ones as Tititl, Stomach Where We Were Born, and Toci, Our Grandmother, Woman of the Wrinkled Uterus. One also notices that the benevolent Yoalticitl (Protector of Children) and Tonantzin (Our Venerated Mother) inhabit the same poetic space as the more terrifying Tzizimicihuatl (Infernal Mother) and Yaocihuatl (Warrior Woman). This tendency to tolerate contradictions, to bridge dichotomies, is a principal characteristic of the mestiza consciousness. In fact, the Virgin is named "Dark Goddess of Duality," and Anzaldúa makes this point too in reference to Coatlicue: "Like Medusa, the Gorgon, she is a symbol of the fusion of opposites: the eagle and the serpent, heaven and the underworld, life and death, mobility and immobility, beauty and horror" (p. 69).

NAOMI QUIÑONEZ is the second poet of Mexican origin who writes from the heart of Aztlán. For Quiñonez this desert landscape is a place of spiritual awakening and healing: "Below a Sandia mountain / una curandera me cura / hechicera de amor / who plies my spirit with / gentle orations that sift / like sage smoke through the fingers / of her eyes" ("Returning to Aztlán"). The *curandera* as traditional healer is both priestess and sorceress, a maternal figure that possesses the spiritual wisdom and power of the Pueblo people, a culture whose roots run deep in the indigenous Aztlán. The poem meanders like a mountain river from Spanish to English and back again, and one hears and feels the rhapsode's intensity as the last lines flow into the waters of ecstasy. The poet's final communion with Aztlán takes the form of the Eucharist, though not the conventional wheat wafer of the Host but rather the indigenous corn tortilla. Speaking in her maternal Spanish, the poet sings, "¡Estoy moliendo mi vida, / tortilla de pasión, / la hostia de comunión / con el corazón! / El corazón de Aztlán" (I am grinding my life, / tortilla of passion / the communion host / with the heart! / The heart of Aztlán). Another poem of syncretic spirituality, "To My Grandmothers," contains a prayer to the Aztec Tezcatlipoca, "a creator god, omnipotent and arbitrary," according to Rafael Tena (La religión mexica [Mexico City: Instituto de Antropología e Historia, 1993], p. 26; my translation). Like the poet's grandmothers, Tezcatlipoca is a life giver, a divine guide in times of trouble, a trickster too, the mysterious "keeper of a smoking [obsidian] mirror." The poem concludes in paradox, with the poet invoking this deity of dark reflections for illumination: "Illumine our mirror, / oh Giver of Life. / Like the sun, reflect our light." Indeed, the hybrid consciousness is grounded in paradox; thus, the mestiza develops, according to Anzaldúa, a "tolerance for contradictions, a tolerance for ambiguity" (p. 101).

Mestizo Sacredness: Poets of Caribbean Origin

VÍCTOR HERNÁNDEZ CRUZ, RICHARD BLANCO, and I are three poets of Caribbean origin who explore in different ways the region's cross-cultural spirituality. Several syncretic religions of African origin exist in the Hispanic Caribbean, in particular Cuba, the best known being Santería. Before beginning a discussion of these poets' work, here is a brief introduction to this Afro-Cuban faith.

Like *Candomblé* in Brazil and *Vodun* (voodoo) in Haiti, Cuba's Santería is a religion that fuses elements of Catholic and West

African spirituality, in particular that of the Yoruba people. This syncretism was crucial to its survival in the hostile environment of the Cuban barracoon because it allowed the slaves to secretly worship their divinities, called *orishas* (Yoruba), disguised as Catholic saints. (It is not uncommon to find in the homes of *santeros* five-foot statues of *santos* surrounded by the familiar votary candles and also by pots of cooked food as well as tropical fruits and vegetables such as coconuts and ripe plantains.) By tricking their masters into believing they were praying to, for example, the Virgin Mary or Saint Barbara, rather than Yemayá or Changó, the newly baptized slaves were able to maintain their traditional beliefs even in the midst of terrible oppression and hardship. To this day, because of their courageous and clever resistance to white authority, we find descendants like the Afro-Cuban poet Pedro Pérez Sarduy describing a childhood filled with chants in Lucumí, the Yoruba language as spoken in Cuba. "They came to me at the dinner table, they came to me in bed," he declares. "My grandmother lullabied in this way."

Besides this sacred music, most often played with goat-skin drums (called *batá*) and gongs (*agogo*), Santería encompasses other modes of worship such as animal sacrifice; communal dancing; offerings of food; beaded necklaces worn by devotees; spiritual cleansing by roots, herbs, and other plants; the casting of cowry shells for divination; and elaborate initiation rites. Every *orisha* has his or her favorite food and his or her special *yerbas* (herbs). Each also represents a particular cosmic principle, with its associated number, color, and emblem. Dance is, above all others, the essential mode of worship for *santeros*. Thus, when a believer dances to Yemayá, for example, she feels the *orisha* " riding" her head as she whirls into ecstasy; in other words, this *orisha* of the sea and maternity takes possession of the believer, whose body then becomes a conduit for her spiritual power. Some other important divine possessions include the following, with their relevant attributes and symbolism (the source is Joseph M. Murphy's excellent table in *Santería:*

African Spirits in America [Boston: Beacon Press, 1988, 1993, pp. 42-43]):

1. Changó, *orisha* of fire and lightning, syncretized as Santa Barbara; his color is red; his symbol is the double ax; his favorite food is goat.
2. Elegguá, *orisha* of the crossroads, the way opener, the trickster, syncretized as the Christ Child of Atocha; his colors are red and black; his symbol is the hooked staff; his favorite food is white chicken.
3. Ochún, *orisha* of eros, syncretized as Cuba's patron saint, Our Lady of Charity of Cobre; her color is yellow; her symbols are the fan, gold, and the peacock feather; her favorite food is a white hen, a she-goat, or a ewe.

A native of Puerto Rico who grew up in New York City, VÍCTOR HERNÁNDEZ CRUZ has established himself as one of the principal architects of this poetics of *mestizaje*. Many of his poems strive to create new and vibrant fusions that reflect the Nuyoricans' multicultural heritage (Spanish, Taíno, African, and American). Thus his language is frequently multilingual, exhibiting a euphonious synthesis of Afro-Caribbean and black urban rhythms. A poet with a gift for verbal play, Hernández Cruz can be quite convincing when fashioning images of spiritual ecstasy that are at the same time reverential and irreverent. The following lines from "La Milagrosa" (The Miraculous One) illustrate the point:

> Virgin of the Miracles makes a
> Sandwich of me between the sky
> And the moon . . .
> She pokes her fingers into the silver
> Holes of stars
> Celestial orgasms like squeezing
> Pluto-size cherries over a lemon earth

The poem has the additional complexity of creating an interplay between fire and ice, the former metonymic for the

7

Caribbean and the latter the cold urban north. Similarly playful, "The Physics of Ochún" is a narrative poem about the miraculous tears of the Virgin Mary (syncretized as this Yoruba *orisha*) that illustrates the conflict between science and faith. The humor here is extravagant and theatrical and thus quintessentially Caribbean, reminiscent of writers like Cuba's Severo Sarduy and Puerto Rico's Luis Rafael Sánchez. The poem is a marvelous potage of magical realism and kitsch, *relajo* (joshing) and *cuento* (tall tale).

Dance and song are frequent motifs in the work of this poet. No doubt these are the primary synthesizers of culture not just in the Hispanic Caribbean but also in Iberia proper, specifically Andalusia, where for centuries Muslims, Christians, and Jews lived together in harmony. Of all the regions of Spain, Al-Andalus (its original Arabic name) has special significance for Hernández Cruz because it represents the origins of Caribbean hybridity. This fusion of Afro-Hispanic and Arab cultures receives its most creative evocation in the poem "Islam," where "whirling dervishes . . . spinning into the arms of light" are compared to "Caribbean mambo dancers." With apparent ease, the poet's cross-cultural imagination creates a centrifugal point of synthesis, a cyclone of dance where two cultures fuse harmoniously into a unity of being.

RICHARD BLANCO'S "Los Santos of the Living Room" also revels in its tropicalized hagiographies, as in the following catalogue of household saints: "Santa Susana de las Quinceañeras" (Saint Susanna of Fifteen-Year-Old Debutantes), "santos del café" (saints of Cuban coffee), "sweet saints of the cane," and, most important, "bendito [holy] San Nostalgia." This is the nostalgia of the exile, the most prevalent theme in Cuban American poetry. "Contemplations at the Virgin de la Caridad Cafeteria, Inc." is another poem by Blanco that ruefully recalls the homeland. "I am the brilliant guitar of a tropical morning," the exile sings. He goes on to invoke the *orishas*: "African gods that rule a rhythmic land / playing their music: bongo, *bembé,* conga; / *qué será*, that cast the spells of this rhumba, / this wild birthright, this tropical dance."

Despite the lyrical passion that informs these lines, the place of Africa in Cuban identity is far more complex, however. *Cubanos* of Spanish descent are well known for rejecting Santería while at the same time practicing it. For example, Blanco remembers his mother's words of denial: "Mamá insisted we are not *santero* pagans despite . . . the offerings of glossy apples, the glassfuls of water . . ." ("Los Santos of the Living Room"). Many cubanos are not wholehearted believers but instead embrace only elements of this spirituality for its magical powers. Cuba is a paradox: the most Spanish of all the Caribbean islands, and at the same time among the most African.

My own poems draw inspiration from many literary traditions, such as the metaphysical poetry of Richard Crashaw and John Donne, surrealism, and the magical realism of the Cuban novelist Alejo Carpentier, or, more accurately, *lo real maravilloso,* the marvelously real, a phrase he coined in the preface to his groundbreaking novel *El reino de este mundo* (The Kingdom of This World, 1949). Though I was raised a Roman Catholic in Lima, Peru, where I was born (both my parents Cuban exiles), I have nonetheless found great beauty and depth of humanity in the Way of Ochá, as believers call Santería. For me it represents a vital and dynamic cross-cultural spirituality, one that has nourished my imagination and allowed me to create new poetic textures for representing the sacred.

Though Santería is in itself a syncretic religion, many of my poems create hybridities of my own imagining. For example, in "Doña Flora's Hothouse," the "sheared parts" of saints' bodies "fructify in African soil / from Ilé-Ifé," that kingdom in Yoruba mythology where the *orishas* created mankind. And the vulture Caná-Caná from Santería folklore "flies to heaven carrying / missives, prayer beads and pits." The poem ends with a eucharistic banquet where the "green thumb" hermit Doña Flora eats these saints' fruits with her animal companions.

9

In another poem, titled "The Tropics Reclaim Calvary," I imagine Saint Lazarus "wish[ing] he were / an African god— beautiful, / healthy—who drums / the world enrapturing mortals / and immortals alike." In the Santería pantheon of gods and goddesses, Saint Lazarus happens to be the ever-popular Babalú-Ayé whose emblem is a pair of crutches, and he is prayed to by those seeking miraculous cures.

Another healer is the *orisha* Osaín, the subject of my poem of the same name. Traditionally represented as Saint Joseph, his principle *las yerbas medicinales* (medicinal herbs), his emblem leaves, Osaín is the patron of *curanderos*, traditional healers, and the "Intercessor who never sleeps / keeping vigil over the sick." "Women smear / cocoa butter on the trunk [of a *framboyán*] / imploring . . . [him] to protect their firstborn." Toward the end of the poem this African god is transformed into a Christ figure who "come[s] from Dahomey / where . . . [he] heal[ed] / the lame, blind, and invalids." Wearing "a loincloth of green / tobacco leaves, thorny vines creeping down the legs," Osaín tells the father of a sick girl, whom he later cures, "At Nazareth / I raised Lazarus / from the twice dead. Have faith, / each breath's a miracle."

Shamans and Babaláwos

A native of Colombia, MAURICE KILWEIN GUEVARA frequently adopts the voice of the shaman in his spiritual poetry. His agile, incantatory lines recall the chants of an Amerindian oral tradition now precariously close to oblivion. These poems of homage take us back to a pre-Columbian world of Edenic beauty where "in the darkness of the forest thousands of white flowers [would] prick our eyes like stars" ("River Spirits").

One discovers in Kilwein Guevara's poems a magical world of visions and portents where "Mohammed's Fatima [can appear] in a grain of wild rice" and the First Mother (Eve? Virgin Mary?) can possess "a firefly like the stone of a ring" ("Why Given to Be Adopted").

These are revelations of infinite spiritual possibilities so that "'Christ could be anyone. Anything'" ("Good Friday"). Thus the shaman healer, as Christ figure, can embody all the spiritualities of our Americas. "I am nothing but bone and American song," he says in "I Sing on the Day of the Deceased." He is the heavenly musician who "play[s] turtleback guitar[,] ghost flute[,] conch." The ecstatic shaman chants his many names and powers, a multilingual catalogue of marvelous incarnations. For example, he is the "dogwood flowering pink." He is "the wizened Aleut praying in the Russian Church." He is "Changó el gran putas." He "ride[s] with Edchewe on the perilous journey to the sun and moon."

Generally, these are not poems of conflict and defiance but of peace and fraternity; thus we hear the shaman affirming his brotherhood with Christian missionaries: "O missionaries / we are brothers on the dark road // How many times do I have to tell you" ("Cofradía"). Nevertheless, one poem in particular, "A City Prophet Talks to God on the 56C to Hazelwood," displays a more combative spirituality. Taking on the identity of an inner-city Saint John the Baptist, the shaman rants against injustice and blight, even questioning God himself in language that strikes of nihilism: "You think my brain's polluted . . . I think we're all lice on a fat rat's back." Overall, however, Kilwein Guevara's poems are testaments to faith and courage; the shaman healer is a life-affirming figure who acts as protector, as guide to the mysteries of existence. "Listen to the sound of rain on stone," he says. "The flute I blow / was once that happy arm that held you in the dark."

Of mixed Dominican and Cuban heritage, ADRIÁN CASTRO is a practitioner of Santería. In fact, he is a *babaláwo,* a high priest who has been initiated into the sacred art of Yoruba divination, called *Ifá.* (You will find his essay in Appendix B extremely informative; it is the only one I know written from an insider's point of view.) As a poet, Castro is unusually cognizant of his Afro-Caribbean heritage. For example, "The Mysteries Come to the Bridge" is a visionary poem that mythically bridges

Afro-Cuba and *Vodun* Haiti. One can read it as a prayer against forgetting ancestral Africa. Even the fish "are wise because they witness and remember / Ochún quien es [who is] Ezuli / Ogún es Ogu . . . Loko es Iróko." Another poem that concerns itself with Mother Africa is "Para la Installation de José Bedia." The speaker (as communal voice) emphasizes his resistance against forgetting, against the erasure of diasporic memory. "Gathering bits of myth" is an act that bonds the children of Africa, that "provoke[s] stability and peace of mind." Like that of his predecessor Hernández Cruz, Castro's language is fluidly heteroglossic, a New World sacred tongue that combines Yoruba, Spanish, English, and Taíno into a harmonious synthesis. Indeed, water is one of the primordial liquids (along with blood) of Santería sacredness, and references to it are numerous in Castro's poetry. Though the Middle Passage took place in water, it is paradoxically water that inspires the poet to imagine a return to Africa.

Los Católicos: Latino Catholics

Up to now the discussion has focused principally on syncretic or non-Western spiritualities of one kind or another that took root in Latin America, but one should not forget that Catholicism is the unquestioned faith of most Latinos. Five poets who explore this rich spiritual life from various perspectives are Benjamín Alire Sáenz, Diana Rivera, Pat Mora, Demetria Martínez, and Virgil Suárez.

A native of New Mexico, BENJAMÍN ALIRE SÁENZ addresses themes dear to Catholics of Mexican origin, as well as other Latinos: Easter, a child's first communion, *los muertos* (the deceased), El Niño Jesús (the Christ Child), and the crucifixion, as well as more scriptural topics such as the Wedding Feast at Cana and the Miracle in the Garden. Sáenz's poems are rooted *en su tierra*, the land of his birth, many years before the reforms of Vatican Council II—a time when choirboys sounded like "ragged / notes from ragged angels' voices; / ancient hymns sung in crooked Latin" ("Easter"). This former Jesuit priest lived for many years away from home, yet his poems show that he never really left the community of Hispanos where he grew up, where people continued to cling to their religious traditions inherited from colonial Mexico. Even after the Southwest was conquered by the United States in 1848, these communities resisted assimilation, and still to this day one finds Hispanos practicing rituals and devotions that date back to fifteenth-century Spain. These lines from the poem "Sacrifices" speak to this legacy: "Today, we take our place, follow / The path that has been worn down by the generations before us / To make our travels lighter."

As the theologian Roberto S. Goizueta has observed in his book *Caminemos con Jesús: Toward a Hispanic/Latino Theology of Accompaniment* (Maryknoll, NY: Orbis Books, 1995, p. 48), "one of the central aspects of Latino popular Catholicism is its incarnational character . . . [thus] . . . religious statues or figures [of Jesus and Mary] are not mere representations of a reality completely external to them." On the contrary, these objects become "the concrete embodiment, in time and space, of Jesus and Mary." Therefore, the image of El Niño Jesús is not a symbol but the very presence of the incarnation. These lines from "The Adoration of the Infant Jesus" illustrate a personal and affective spiritual relationship between the believer and the sacred object: "When my lips reach / His feet, he will turn to flesh . . . He is alive . . . we who have kissed him know that he is real." Also, when the poet's cherished clay crucifix accidentally breaks, he repairs it with great care and devotion: "I will kneel, reglue it, / transform it once again. It will hang forever on my wall" ("Crucifix"). For him it is a living symbol of the resurrection, as alive as the Host of the Eucharist, and in "Sacrifices" the poet remembers with awe the first time he "tasted the Catholic God [. . . ,] his tongue still tingling from the touch of the white host."

Sáenz's poetry also attests to the importance of the Latino family in transmitting religious beliefs. Once controlled by clerics of Irish and German descent, the U.S. Catholic Church had a long history of marginalizing Latino communities. Few priests could, or cared to, speak Spanish, and they scorned Latino beliefs and traditions as being either naive or medieval. *La familia* inevitably had to take on a more dominant role than would have been the case in Latin America. This neglect created a situation where the priest had no absolute dominion; thus the poet's *abuelita* is able to explain the resurrection with tender authority: " 'The dead / will rise.' She moved her hands toward me, / wrapped my face with touches, and / laughed again. *The dead will rise*" ("Easter"). Though the poem has her speaking in English, Spanish is the language of the home, which often takes on maternal significance: "[I felt] safer—protected in the warmth / Of Spanish" ("Adoration of the Infant Jesus").

Sáenz's devotional poetics also deserves consideration. For example, we find the brilliant "To the Desert," a meditation inspired by Donne's famous Holy Sonnet 14. In apostrophic lines, the poet imagines the desert as a divine entity that has the majestic and absolute power of Donne's Trinitarian God, his verbs alliterative hammerings: "You reach—then *bend / Your force, to break, blow, burn, and make me new*" (his italics). The poem concludes with a moving and imaginative self-consecration in which the penitent imagines himself as the desert's "bread" (flesh, host) and "water" (blood, wine). "*Salva, traga,*" he exclaims. Save me, swallow me.

A native of Puerto Rico, DIANA RIVERA also writes meditations that suggest the influence of Donne and other seventeenth-century English devotional poets. Unlike Sáenz, her appropriation of Donne's idiom indicates more of an attraction to mortification than to sacramental ecstasies: "Pierce me! Spades and hooks, / pluck this forlorn mood, / yank the bitter outlook, the dark aneurysm / in my looming sky" ("Prayer"). (Another vivid trope from the same poem is "storm-cabbaged soul," a strange, though striking, locution that sounds like a cross between the hermetic Henry Vaughan and the surrealist Aimé Cesaire.) The poem called "Healing," however, evokes God in more positive and idealistic terms. The dominant conceit here is of God as divine physician who "pours a strange light . . . brightening wounds . . . who pours the healing graces until we believe in God again." Contrary to what a Donnean poetics would dictate, Rivera's imagination emphasizes nurturing and healing rather than brilliant rhetoric and polemical theology. Above all, Rivera's spiritual poems speak to God's love in one way or another, and these lines from "Luminous Moon" communicate the mystery of divine love with ethereal clarity: "It's soothing to hear / the wings of light envelop us, / to feel the infinite protection, / the incomprehensible / pulsing love of God."

Writing in the voice of an elderly Aunt Carmen, a church sacristan, PAT MORA speaks to the saints in plain yet musical language. Her prayers are intimate and candid, her entreaties passionate, her questioning forthright, her metaphors delicate and resonant. Their charm lies in their folksy wisdom, their traditional rhythms. Addressing Saint Martin of Porres, a mulatto born in sixteenth-century Peru who is patron saint of racial relations, she implores him to "cease wrinkled judgments based on skin, / our colored sacks like bulbs or seeds / that hold our fragrant selves within."

On the other hand, the voice we hear in DEMETRIA MARTÍNEZ'S "Psalm" is one that has strayed from God, and the psalmist struggles to regain her Christian faith in a materialistic world that denies the very existence of mystical experience "as just a tap dance of neurotransmitters."

Concluding this section are three poems by the Cuban American VIRGIL SUÁREZ inspired by his childhood in Havana and Madrid. For example, "The Nuns in the Family" is a tongue-in-cheek story about a bull run amok and how his two aunts, nuns "dressed like *urracas* [magpies]," were miraculously saved from being gored. Another is a rich and vivid description of the San Lázaro procession in Havana. And though the poet confesses he is no believer in religion, he nonetheless recalls (or perhaps just imagines) a strange and powerful vision of his Sunday school teacher, Sister Nola, naked and red-haloed, holding the crucifix he had made from clothespins, which burned with "a glow so bright [he] believed the sun had swallowed [them] both" ("Clothespins/Los palitos de tendederas").

Alternate Spiritualities:
Beauty and Nature as Realms of Sacredness

The poets in this category are perhaps the most innovative of the anthology, for they are discovering and mapping new spiritual landscapes for Latinos. RICHARD BLANCO'S recent poetry exhibits a shift away from the spiritualized nostalgia of exile found in "Los Santos of the Living Room" to a more radical consideration of the sacred vis-à-vis the physical world. For instance, his poem titled "Relativity," inspired by Einstein's theory, meditates on the relationship between mind and matter. The poet presents us with images of mutability, telling us that "absolutely nothing is ever absolutely still." In such a world of change—with its cycles of birth and death, growth and decay, creation and destruction—physical bodies, though beautiful and substantial, ultimately "hurl" toward the inevitable chaos—the hell—of "irreconcilable pieces." Only the mind can escape mutability, only the mind is able to "reach for the speed of light." The poet commands us to "accelerate / and warp the mind a little mile after mile / per second per second per ever per ever." Therefore, one can conjecture that as it escapes faster and faster from this chaos, from this void, the mind propels itself toward an ecstatic state of pure light.

A similarly kinetic poem is DIONISIO MARTÍNEZ'S "Ash Wednesday," a complex meditation on Michelangelo's famous *Creation of Adam,* one of the nine main biblical scenes he painted on the ceiling of the Sistine Chapel. Here and elsewhere this Cuban American poet's spirituality is individualistic and elusive, and the closest thing to a label might be something like aesthetic agnosticism. However, this lyric essay does transcend doubt and achieves, even if fleetingly, an affirmation of the divine presence, the speaker employing a paradoxical logic whose "movement away from something is movement toward something."

A second poet whose understanding of the sacred cannot be divorced from aesthetics is VALERIE MARTÍNEZ, a Mexican American. In her beautiful poem "Tesoro" (Treasure), Martínez laments the death of loved ones and initially considers sacred art, specifically "the façades of the Sagrada Familia with their delicate foliage," as her one source of consolation against this world of death and change. "It was my treasure," she declares, "this permanence, the architecture of living." However, the poet goes on to reconsider this assertion, acknowledging the "mistake" of her perception, for though the handmaid in *The Visitation* is made "real" (incarnate) by the artist's gifted hand, she is nonetheless "impermanent." Only the imagination, her true "*tesoro*," allows the poet to "reach out toward the substantial, to the place where they've [the dead] all gone."

Another poem devoted to the memory of the dead is "Invocation," whose rhapsodic chanting evokes a sacredness older than Christianity, a spirituality that recalls the sibylline songs of the ancients. Though the poem's setting is the Mexican Day of the Dead, one feels reluctant to reduce it to some Amerindian spirituality. The speaker can either be an Aztec priest(ess), a Roman *vates* (poet-prophet), a Greek sybil, or for that matter all three. The poem's spirituality is thus more universal and thereby resistant to categorization. Ultimately, it leads us to an apprehension of the sacral beauty of the dead, who "are moonstone," "hollow stone," "mist on the bones / in mother-of-pearl."

Cuban-born ALEIDA RODRÍGUEZ'S spiritual poems push the boundaries of what constitutes a communion with the divine. "What the Water Gave Me," for instance, evokes in ecstatic language the divinity of nature, specifically water, which is "baptismal, disastrous, transformative." Regardless of our technological and engineering breakthroughs, human beings cannot control water. The more spiritual alternative, something that ancient peoples understood, is for us to live in harmony with it, knowing that the "watery will reshapes history, obliterates evidence, gets its own way." Just as we cannot command God to do our bidding, we cannot pray water "forward, down, toward calm. No such luck." Its life-giving properties cannot be divorced from its power to destroy. It is like Jehovah, the Creator and Destroyer, He who both gave life and took life. Therefore, we must learn to *Let it go, let it go, go, go,*" as "the water angel says."

Besides this excursion into what might be termed pantheism, Rodríguez also explores the sacramental possibilities of the human body in her poem "The Invisible Body," with its long, sinuous lines. This invisible body is worshipped "like an old-fashioned lover, from afar," the speaker asserts. "It's more than prayer it wants—more than language. . . . [It] . . . demands [that] you invent new senses to receive it." Is this invisible body the soul, the other self, the angel within us, the divine seed? The poem does not say. It could be one, all, or none. One invisible body is not like any other. It cannot be measured. It is elusive yet intimate at the same time. To know what the invisible body is we must follow our spiritual intuition, the divine voice within us.

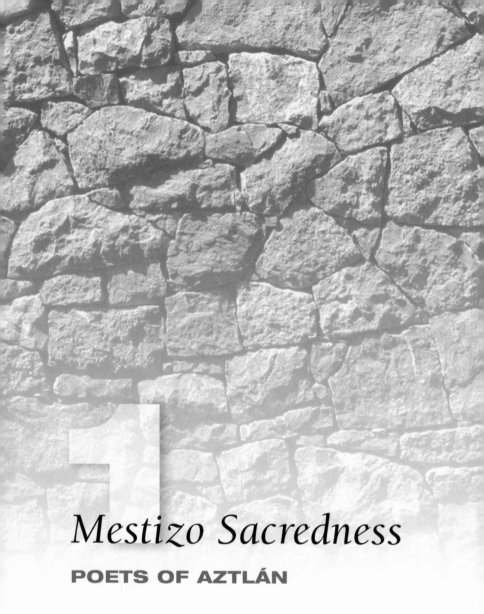

1

Mestizo Sacredness

POETS OF AZTLÁN

Pat Mora

Consejos de Nuestra Señora de Guadalupe: Counsel from the Brown Virgin

You seem surprised that I've appeared.
You gape like Juan Diego as I hovered in a cloud
that December morning above dry Tepeyac. Mortals lack faith
and imagination, fear flying. Hijas, be unpredictable.

> Como la flor de rosa.
> Como el arco iris.
> Como las nubes de gloria.
> Como la luna espléndida.

Do not be insistent. I raise neither my voice nor eyes—
yet. Bodies, even celestial, are creatures of habit.
Hijas, what we repeat becomes our nature. Beware.
Goddesses fade in and out of fashion.

> Como la flor de rosa.
> Como el arco iris.
> Como las nubes de gloria.
> Como la luna espléndida.

Names and images are converted. Now I'm moon-rider
in repose, body concealed in flowing cocoon,
hands, mouth, eyes folded, cloaked in stars.
Hijas, consistent trappings can release us for internal work.

> Como la flor de rosa.
> Como el arco iris.
> Como las nubes de gloria.
> Como la luna espléndida.

You analyze the persistence of my image, how I don't fade.
Too much analysis inhibits wisdom, hijas. You fear
flying. A muse amused, I am used everywhere, auto-shops,
buses, bars, slender mother but virgen pura, no Malinche.

> Como la flor de rosa.
> Como el arco iris.
> Como las nubes de gloria.
> Como la luna espléndida.

Hijas, beware of altars and rumors of legends.
Holy men altered me, Aztec goddess to Reina de Las Américas,
pyramid to cathedral. They say I called sweet as birdsong
to Juan Diego rushing to the curling hum of holy incense.

> Como la flor de rosa.
> Como el arco iris.
> Como las nubes de gloria.
> Como la luna espléndida.

Send men clear signs. They need them, hijas.
In deserts, I favor scarlet roses. Come.
Rise. Practice solitary levitation. Rise,
but ignore halos, hovering men who look like angelitos.

> Como la flor de rosa.
> Como el arco iris.
> Como las nubes de gloria.
> Como la luna espléndida.

Hijas, value contemplation. Alone, I write
my own legends. My lines improve. Play the symbols.
I loan my cape to women in tennis shoes who fly
back and forth across the Río Grande.

> Como la flor de rosa.
> Como el arco iris.
> Como las nubes de gloria.
> Como la luna espléndida.

Listen to this buzz of litanies. Endless praise inhibits musing.
Hijas, silence can be pregnant. My voice rose like a beam
of sunlight, entered Juan. Remember, conceptions,
immaculate and otherwise, happen. He knelt, full of me.

> Como la flor de rosa.
> Como el arco iris.
> Como las nubes de gloria.
> Como la luna espléndida.

Coatlicue's Rules: Advice from an Aztec Goddess

Rule 1: Beware of offers to make you famous.

I, pious Aztec mother lost in housework,
am pedestaled, "She of the Serpent Skirt,"
necklace dangling hearts and hands, faceless
statue, two snakes eye-to-eye on my shoulders,
goddess of earth, also death, which leads to

Rule 2: Retain control of your own publicity.

Past is present. Women are women.
I'm not competitive and motherhood isn't
about numbers, but four hundred sons and a daughter
may be a record even without the baby.
There's something wrong in this world
if a woman isn't safe even when she sweeps
her own house, when any speck can enter even through
the eye, I'll bet, and become a stubborn tenant.

Rule 3: Protect your uterus.

Conceptions, immaculate and otherwise, happen.
Women swallow sacred stones that fill their bellies
with elbows and knees. In Guatemala, a skull dangling
from a tree whispers, "Touch me,"
to a young girl, and a clear drop
drips on her palm, disappears. Dew
drops in, if you know what I mean.
Saliva moved in her, the girl says. Moved in, I say,
settled into that empty space, and grew. Men know.
They stay full of themselves, keeps occupancy down.

Rule 4: Avoid housework.

Remember, I was sweeping, humming, actually,
high on Coatepec, our Serpent Mountain, humming loud
so I wouldn't hear all those sighs inside.
I was sweeping slivers, gold and jade, picking up
after four hundred sons who think they're gods,
and their spoiled sister. I was sweeping
when feathers fell on me, brushed my face,
first light touch in years, like in a dream.

At first, I just blew them off, then I saw
the prettiest ball of tiny plumes, glowing
green and gold. Gently, I gathered it. Oh,
it was soft as baby hair, brought back mother-
shivers when I pressed it to my skin. I nestled it
like I used to nestle them, here,
when they finished nursing. Maybe I even stroked
the roundness. I have since heard that feathers
aren't that unusual at annunciations, but I was innocent.

After sweeping, I looked in vain inside
my clothes, but the soft ball had vanished, well,
descended. I think I showed within the hour,
or so it seemed. They noticed first, of course.

Rule 5: Avoid housework. It bears repeating.

I was too busy washing, cooking, sweeping again,
worrying about my daughter, Painted with Bells,
when I began to bump into their frowns
and mutterings. They kept glancing at my stomach,
started pointing. I got so hurt and mad, I started crying.
Why do they get to us? One wrong word or look
from any one of them doubles me over,
and I've had four hundred and one, no anesthetic.

Near them I'm like a snail with no shell on a sizzling day.
They started yelling, "Wicked, wicked," and my daughter,
right there with them, my wannabe warrior boy.

The yelling was easier than the whispers, "Kill. Kill.
Kill. Kill." Kill me? Their mother?
One against four hundred and one? All I'd done
was press that feathered softness into me.

Rule 6: Listen to inside voices.

You mothers know about the baby in a family, right?
Even if he hadn't talked to me from deep inside,
he would have been special. Maybe the best.
But as my name is Coatlicue, he did.
That unborn child, that started as a ball of feathers
all soft green and gold, heard my woes, and spoke to me.
A thoughtful boy. And formal too. He said, "Do not be afraid,
I know what I must do." So I stopped shaking.

Rule 7: Verify that the inside voice is yours.

I'll spare you the part about the body hacking
and head rolling. But he was provoked, remember.
All this talk of gods and goddesses distorts.

This planet wasn't big enough for all of us,
but my whole family has done well for itself, I think.
I'm the mother of stars. My daughter's white head
rolls round the heavens each night, and my sons
wink down at me. What can I say—a family
of high visibility. The baby? Up there also, the sun,
the real thing. Such a god he is, of war unfortunately,
and the boy never stops, always racing across the sky,
every day of the year, a ball of fire since birth.

But I think he has forgotten me. You sense my ambivalence.
I'm blinded by his light.

Rule 8: Insist on personal interviews.

Past is present, remember. Men carved me,
wrote my story, and Eve's, Malinche's, Guadalupe's,
Llorona's, snakes everywhere, even in our mouths.

Rule 9: Be selective about what you swallow.

Litany to the Dark Goddess

Coatlicue, Mother of All Gods,
Coatlicue, She of the Serpent Skirt,
Coatlicue, Goddess of Earth, Life, Death,
Coatlicue of Coatepec,
Teteoian, Mother of the Gods, Mother of Four Hundred
    Thousand,
Tlaliyolo, Heart of the Earth, Blood Giver and Blood Taker,
Tititl, Stomach Where We Were Born,
Omecihuatl, Lady of Duality,
Cihuacoatl, Woman Serpent, She of the Windowless Temple,
Yoalticitl, Goddess of Cradles, Protector of Children,
Cuaucihuatl, Eagle Woman, Woman of Claws,
Yaocihuatl, Warrior Woman, Woman of Unflinching Gaze,
Quilaztli, Sorceress, Transformer into Animals,
Toci, Our Grandmother, Woman of Wrinkled Uterus,
Teotenantzin, Beloved Mother of the Gods,
Tzizimicihuatl, Infernal Mother,
Tonantzin, Our Venerated Mother,
Tonantzin of Tepeyac, Patroness of Midwives and Healers,
Virgin
Virgin of Tepeyac, Virgin of Guadalupe,
Virgin of Roses the Color of Blood,
Goddess Who Fears No Serpent,
Goddess Who Floats on the Moon,
Goddess of Folded Hands, Goddess of Folded Body,
Hidden Goddess,
Dark Goddess of Duality,
Coatlicue, Tonantzin, Guadalupe,
Silent Pedestal Goddess,
Colonized Goddess,
Goddess of Downcast Eyes,
María full of sorrows,
Santa María llena de gracia,

Virgin of Virgins,
Mother Most Pure,
Intact Mother,
Spotless Mother,
Santísima Virgen,
Spiritual Vessel,
Tower of Marble,
Rosa Mística,
House of Gold,
Morning Star,
Dulce Madre,
Mother of Mothers,
Mother of Hope,
María de Miel,
Despierta.
Dreamer of Your Many Manifestations,
Despierta.
Dreamer of Fierce Origins,
Despierta. Óyenos.
Claw through their babble,
we're straining to hear.

Naomi Quiñonez

Returning to Aztlán

Upon a return from a return
regresando de tiempos
rasguñados, líneas finas, moradas
venas de manos antiguas.
Poder.
That is the name
of this dress I wear
as I skirt along the sides
of open highways,
tasting moist mouthfuls
of desert wind.
I run roads—the roadrunner
traversing state lines—
faldas unfold like waves
upon the shores of Albuquerque
the tips of the Picuris.
With open veins I take in
the shadows of hummingbirds,
feathered fusion
of small beating wings
on the back porch of my travels.
Dusty journey through
corn blue skies, ojos calientes,
labios picantes,
volcanes muertos,
smoking in ancient petroglyphs
of familiar faces.
La poesía de los pueblos
me sigue: Española, Taos y Santa Fe,
las Truchas, Barelas y Chimayó,

las Trampas, Belén y Bernalillo.
My belly is full with Burque stew,
blue homilies of corn
in a thick sauce
of red and green desire.
With full heart I visit
el artista in his kiva
of ill-repute
where I contemplate a silver head
upon a severed plate.
He serves bold metaphors for dinner
and his friends must have
large appetites.
Below a Sandia mountain
una curandera me cura
hechicera de amor
who plies my spirit with
gentle orations that sift
like sage smoke through the fingers
of her eyes.
Ay más, y más
ay masa hecho dentro
de la curva ancha
de mi molcajete.
¡Estoy moliendo mi vida,
tortilla de pasión,
la hostia de comunión
con el corazón!
El corazón de Aztlán.

To My Grandmothers

(Your voices guide my heart, my pen.)

Is this the time of Tezcatlipoca,
keeper of the smoking mirror,
Nahuatl trickster, divine guide?
Is this the time of obscured hearts and faces?
With idle illusions we adorn our fears,
with masks we hide our greed.
Is this how he makes us his?
Without pure hearts or a true face
the mirror remains clouded.
Will we be the inheritors of smoke?
Illumine our mirror, oh Giver of Life.
Like the sun, reflect our light!

—in tribute to the Nahuatl poets

Good Friday

Sage smoke circles
like a phantom
around my head.
Morning offering
unbridled thought
merge while muse
speaks softly to me
on this my good Friday.
Noon bells toll
it is the hour of sacrifice
to reflect on those crosses
large and small
I have carried.
This death is like a lover
a mad moment of passion
abandon and disintegration.
Blood and tears
are from the same source
they are the shadows of wounds
no one can see.
This death is like
a woman's labor
pain, wreathing
relief and joy.
On this my good Friday
I do penance on paper
and work my way to a rebirth
free of reason.
On this my good Friday
I treasure the tree of life
and give thanks
for the journey
and the destination.

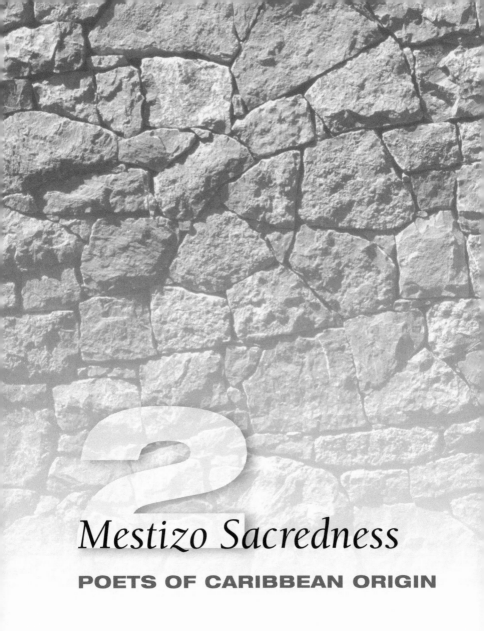

2

Mestizo Sacredness

POETS OF CARIBBEAN ORIGIN

Víctor Hernández Cruz

The Physics of Ochún

A group of professional
scientists
from Columbia University
heard that in an old
tenement apartment
occupied by a family
named González
a plaster-of-Paris
statue made in Rome
of Caridad del Cobre
started crying
The scientists
curious as they are
took a ride across
town to investigate
After stating their purpose
and their amazement
they were led to the
room where the statue was
Sure enough it was wet
under the eyes
Overnight, Señora González
told them, it had cried so
much that they were able
to collect a jar full of tears
The scientist almost knocked his
gold-rim glasses off his face
May we have this as a specimen
to study in our laboratory?
She agreed, and they took a taxi

with the jar to Columbia
They went directly to the lab
to put the tears through a
series of tests
They put a good amount of
the liquid under their
Strongest Microscope
Lo and behold!
What they saw made them loosen
their neckties
There inside the liquid
clearly made out through
the microscope was the
word: JEHOVAH
No matter how much they
moved the water they
kept getting the word
They sent for a bottle of
scotch
They served themselves in test tubes
They called the González family
to see if they could explain
All the González family knew
was that it was the tears
of Caridad del Cobre
They explained to Señora González
what was happening
She said that weirder than that
was the fact that her
window had grown a staircase
that went up beyond the clouds
She said she and her daughter
had gone up there to check it
out
because, she told them, a
long white rope had come out

of their belly buttons and some-
thing was pulling them up
What happened? the enthusiastic
scientists from Columbia University
wanted to know
We went up there and were
massaged by the wind
We got hair permanents
and our nails manicured
looking a purple red
My daughter says she saw
a woodpecker designing the
air
The scientists put the phone down
and their eyes orbited the room
We have to get out there
Incredible things are happening
They rushed back out
and into the González residency
They entered
It's in the same
room with the statue
They rushed in and went to the
window
So amazed were they
they lost their speech
All their organs migrated an inch
Clearly in front of them
a 3-foot-wide marble stair
which went up into the sky
The scientists gathered themselves
to the point of verbalizing again
They each wanted to make sure
that the other was "cognizant"
of the *espectáculo*
Once they settled upon reality

they decided that the urge to
explore was stronger than their
fears
One decided to take a writing pad
to take notes
One decided to take a test tube
in case he ran into substances
One decided to take a thermometer
and an air bag to collect atmosphere
Señora González, would you please
come up with us?
They wanted to know if she would
lead them up
If you could see it you could touch
it, she told them
She went out first and they
followed
The marble steps were cold
They could have been teeth of
the moon
As they went up the breeze smiled
against their ears
The murmur of the streets dimmed
They were climbing and climbing
when they felt a whirlpool in
the air
For sure it was the hairdresser
Señora González sensed the odor of
many flowers in the breeze
The scientist with the test tube
saw it get full of a white liquid
The scientist with the air bag
felt it change into a chunk of metal
The scientist with the writing pad
saw a language appear on it backwards
printing faster than a computer

40

The paper got hot like a piece of
burning wood
and he dropped it down into the
buildings
It went through an open window
and fell into a pot of red beans
A woman by the name Concepción was
cooking
Frightened she took it to a doctor's
appointment she had the next day
She showed it to the physician
who examined it
He thought it was the imprint
of flower petals
so even and bold in lilac
ink
The dream Concepción had during
the night came back to her
I know what's going on, doctor
I'll see you in nine months
Walking she remembered forgetting
to put the *calabaza* into the beans
and rushed home sparkling in
her yellow dress

La Milagrosa

As red as her lips were she wasn't there
The lonely night like a hidden moon crater
Which wouldn't be there if it were not for eyes
So look at the assembly of fire escapes
High up like on some kind of Ferris wheel
Hearing now footsteps inside the wax of the
Candle which burns for La Milagrosa
Go down the street to see *maniobras*
On the way back the gargoyle that protects
The entrance started talking:
The tops of heads have clear holes
I been spitting rainbows into them for
100 years tonight the half-baked moon
Is there I can breathe it with my nose
Which says the moon is full every day
All the time the moon is out and all
There full like your head in a dream
Close the windows
Aren't those the words of a song humming?
The street turns into soup
Her lips kiss the candle's fire
She walks open my walls
The sky is what I eat with my mouth
Virgin of the Miracles makes a
Sandwich of me between the sky
And the moon
Loneliness is yesterday's newspaper
She pokes her fingers into the silver
Holes of stars
Celestial orgasms like squeezing
Pluto-size cherries over a lemon earth
Roses clean their feet with the face
Of the gargoyle which looks onto the stoop

As red as her lips become blue
Like the mouth of an Alaskan glacier
La Milagrosa leaves footprints on my mind
She leaves stains on the goatskin drums
She leaves the odor of wax
She leaves the fire burning
She is gone from where she never came to
What you hear is only the song maker's
Humming
The street is deserted and covered with ice
The ice that used to be fire

Christianity

Christianity
sparkling from pentecostal
Rhythm
Coming as if a mouth
Up from
Calle San Lázaro del Medio
Timbal and maraca with
tambourine inviting San Pedro
Horse to gallop
Through hair and flesh
Like needles of chill
Pulling down Jehovah
with a singsong
Those beautiful faces that
I saw bopping a wooden church
Gone was the whole place
With white dresses—guayaberas
of grace
Out towards doubtless space
I threw myself in with that
and kneeled next to a picture
Of María with a child
In her arms
A maternal embrace
Taking care of you.

Islam

The revelation of the revelation
The secrets offered in rhythms
The truth of heaven entering through
chorus
Yourself runs into yourself
Through a crack of understanding
As if falcons landed on a
shoulder of your thoughts
With a letter from your guardian
angel—
Like Caribbean mambo dancers
The dervishes go off
spinning into the arms of light
Across a floor of endless squares
and circles
Calligraphy brushed into tiles
Painted inside the names of God
Love
Compassion.

Richard Blanco

Los Santos of the Living Room

At her *Quinces* ball, my cousin Susana was presented to society
as a lavish pearl, unveiled from a giant enameled oyster rolled
right into the center of the festivities. The commemorative
portrait of the fifteen-year-old debutante—caped in feathers,
coyly posed with cherubs at her feet on the marble staircases
of Vizcaya Palace and wisping an Andalusian fan—hung
conspicuously in our living room, competing with the velvet
furniture, the avocado marquise curtains and crème chiffon
sheers. Mamá also hung flea market oil paintings of palm tree
landscapes and ink sketches of La Habana Vieja—La Catedral,
El Capitolio, El Morro. In the china cabinet: souvenir plates
and toothpick holders from Niagara Falls, a miniature flamenco
doll with authentic ivory comb and stomping shoes, fine
porcelain espresso *tacitas* with etched vine roses used only for
high entertaining, a few genuine Lladró figurines glazed in
trademark shades of strict gray-blues, and *los santos:*

Santa Bárbara, 14 inches high with a gold-plated chalice and
halo, a spade in her right hand ready to lance evil, mounted
sidesaddle on her majestic horse; San Lázaro the crippled
leper, glassy eyed, caped in purple velvet, the wire armature
showing through broken-off fingers and toes; and the patron
of the homeland—La Virgen de la Caridad del Cobre—floating
above a mystic sea, protecting our island. Mamá insisted we
are not santero pagans despite the votive candles and the
offerings of glossy apples, the glassfuls of water, the bowls of
hard candies and copper pennies I would steal from the
saints, and the lit *tabaco* smoke swirling with prayer: *Santa
Bárbara bendita, san velvet, san chiffon, Our Lady of the Oyster,*

Santa Susana de las Quinceañeras, santos del flamenco fire, Holy Havana, San Lladró y santísimo San Lázaro, santos del café, sweet saints of the cane, royal santos of las palmas, bendito San Nostalgia, spirit of our fathers and protector of our perpetual dreaming—pray for us, save us, deliver us, return us.

Contemplations at the Virgin
de la Caridad Cafeteria, Inc.

Qué será, el café of this holy, incorporated place,
the wild steam of scorched espresso cakes rising
like mirages from the aromatic waste, waving
over the coffee-glossed lips of these faces

assembled for a standing breakfast of nostalgia,
of tastes that swirl with the delicacy of memories
in these forty-cent cups of brown sugar histories,
in the swirling froth of *café-con-leche, qué será,*

what have they seen that they cannot forget—
the broad-leaf waves of *tabaco* and plantains
the clay dust of red and nameless mountains,
qué será, that this morning I too am a speck;

I am the brilliant guitar of a tropical morning
speaking Spanish and ribboning through potions
of waist-high steam and green cane oceans,
qué será, drums vanishing and returning,

the African gods that rule a rhythmic land
playing their music: bongo, *bembé,* conga;
qué será, that cast the spells of this rumba,
this wild birthright, this tropical dance

with the palms of this exotic confusion;
qué será, that I too should be a question,
qué será, what have I seen, what do I know—
culture of café and loss, this place I call home.

Orlando Ricardo Menes

Doña Flora's Hothouse

The Sargasso Sea in cyclone
season, a flotilla of blessèd corpses
drifting in equatorial currents,
their shaved heads crowned with laurel
to repel lightning, sargassum fronds
swathing both neck and limb.

Tiny crabs burrow ears
oozing cerumen, pipefish slither
into sutured wounds that coffer
bones of African St. Barbara.

In the tropics the blessèd are incorruptible,
whether Goa, Malabo, or Hispaniola.
Landfall at Doña Flora's island
(longitude of Gonave and Barbuda),
green thumb hermit who cultivates

their bodies in a hothouse by the sea.
Sheared parts fructify in African soil
from Ilé-Ifé, guano of Caná-Caná
vulture that flies to heaven carrying
missives, prayer beads and pits.

Swinging her calabash censer,
Doña Flora fumigates with sarsaparilla
entrails of tamarind, soursop kidneys,
banana toes; a *zunzuncito* hummingbird
flies out her ear to sip balsam tears.

Suspended amid laelia orchids
mulatto cherubs trumpet *sones*
from Oriente, Doña Flora rattles

her maraca to sprinkle *aguardiente*
on guava bladders, uteri of red
papaya, mango hearts. By white

mangroves a shanty of lignum vitae,
dried thatching, barnacled crosses.
All Soul's Day and Doña Flora enters
with her animals, laying overripe fruits

on whitest linen. Iguanas chew
sweet-acid tamarind, a *jutía* rat
nibbles guava, Caná-Caná rips papaya—
seeds bursting out—as Doña Flora skins

a mango, bruised with machete,
lifts the bleeding fruit to bands
of amber light, sweet flesh dissolving
in her mouth, its bare stone returned to sea.

Requiem Shark with Lilies

Sailor boy in pantaloons guides his jacaranda
caravel through a labyrinth
of skulls, lichens bleeding in fontanels,
Easter winds
spraying heliotropes with ammonia.
Another makes a halo
stirring sand in brine that has preserved
a martyr's spleen 1,000 years.

St. Agnes sweeps the beach with coco fronds
collecting crossfish,
aureole urchins, angels' quills.
Jumps over a small requiem shark
half buried in wet sand:
its transparent body barbed with diamonds,
ten lilies suspended inside a glass

womb. Breaking the membrane with a weathered
pelican's beak, she tingles
as formaldehyde spills
down to her calcareous toes. One flower
begins to dig a burrow,

flailing iridescent petals very fast.
St. Agnes snatches the lily,
putting it in her clenched hand, which secretes
burning nectar through
the pistil; two stamens—long, spiculed—
squeeze her ring finger until it's blue.

She shakes her hand furiously,
its grip becomes tighter, the horny-beaked
stigma punctures
her fingertip, implants black ovules

that mix with her own blood
as it shoots over breakers. Gust shatters the arc,

the lily dies; rainbow droplets coagulate
coating seeds that germinate
inside fish bellies, alive in purgatory's trenches,
then migrate home with their hosts
at the start of Lent and breed on Easter Sunday.

God's Veins

St. Peter Claver sleeps on nests of great blue heron
                              —fish eggs shimmering
                              in standing holy water—
a smoked sardine tied between
each armpit (*to keep Beelzebub away*) his bed's legs mangrove
    roots that extend

all the way to Aruba; from there capillaries
                              radiate to Curaçao, Bonaire, and all
                              Windward Islands, the most
                                            defenseless
against storms: *God's veins* he tells his African
converts *stronger than nkisi*—fetish—*of Noah's cypress ark*
                              or Eden's kapok,
tree of life St. Peter Claver preaches all over Cartagena
the wheel is Satan's invention: *Only by walking*
                  will we ever enter the New Jerusalem

Hates paper, books, printing press, ink, quills
        (*works of man, ungodly things*) his supplications scratched
on leathery pitch-apple leaves that ferment in *chicha*
                              Lent's purple-maize liquor.

Brine rains down Cartagena.
Bells toll Stations of the Cross.
                              Ten Africans, men and women,
all christened George, are brought
in chains
to hear St. Peter Claver's catechism: *Be devout in all things*
                              bathe daily with your own tongues
        eat only fish, just the heads
                  drink salt water at morning, especially if ill

Demonstrates how the crucifix has everyday uses: anchor, bow,
                  scratcher, digging stick, knocker, hone, hammer

53

The Africans laugh. *Labor is godly* he scolds
even Christ would hammer his own cross, nail his own hands and feet
                                    with a crucifix

Makes them whistle, a few sound like birds.

Only a short S *separates* pecado *from* pescado—sin from fish—
                    Don't ever omit that S, *hell awaits if you do*
Make it very long, sibilant, never hissing, so that you lose your
  breath in rapture

Osaín

Herbalist and *curandero,*
cigar maker to Santería gods, Silvio dries
maduro skins harvested
in darkness—new moon—to prevent holes, blemishes,
any weakening of *ashé*—life force.

                                  Three coronas burn in wood
candlesticks, carved Ibo seraphim;
Silvio pours Haitian cane liquor into sequined shot glasses,
rolls tobacco *cucuruchos*—
cones—stuffing them with possum livers,
                offerings to Osaín, Patron of *curanderos*
                Intercessor who never sleeps
                keeping vigil over the sick.
This *orisha* sprang
from Africa's humus—no seed, a cutting of God's ulna—
without genitals, other body parts;
taught Adam and Eve
which wild plants were medicinal, which mortal;
preached obedience.
                Doesn't dance or sing.

The village *framboyán*—Madagascar flame tree—
has bloomed early
presaging death of children; women smear
cocoa butter on the trunk
imploring Osaín to protect their firstborn.

                Silvio and Tin Tin Tamacún,
his 20-pound calico,
prowl the canebrakes stalking *chichereku* dolls—
amphibious, two-headed,
serrated teeth—who drown children
in frogponds and arroyos, snatching their pure souls

for Kongo master's sorcery.
Silvio's own daughter lies
in a muddy ditch—paralyzed, blind, delirious—
Tamacún pursues the evil spirit
into a patch of weeds, kills the doll
     of ficus wood and cotton braids; Silvio sets it on fire

with kerosene. The girl's fever increases,
jaw locks, bite wounds
suppurate. Silvio tries many cures:
               rum infusion of *okro* seed
               spirit-weed
               decoction, sousumba tea
               tulula-leaf juice
Nothing works.
She begins wheezing, tongue charcoal-black.

          A man crawls out the red earth
beneath *framboyán,*
limps on a forked cross, loincloth of green
tobacco leaves, thorny vines
creeping down the legs; he's missing a foot,
an arm, the left eye.

          I come from Dahomey
where I heal
the lame, blind, and invalids;
          at Nazareth
I raised Lazarus
from the twice dead. Have faith,
each breath's a miracle.
          He rubs the girl's eyes,
          wounds with saliva.
Rise.

Fish Heads

A glowing crucifix (five
flashing lights) atop the lobster trap,
a rosary of papaya seeds,
a clock like a flaming heart
that shudders every hour;
the heart speaks: *I thirst,
It is finished, etc.*

The fisher's son, an acolyte,
sleeps cuddled up in his canoe
of mist, rocking like censer
or bell buoy. Child of the sea,
river, lagoon—Antillean *querubín,*
who drools rose water on the pillow,
commands dolphin and barracuda
to weave arabesques of crown, cross, and pike,
boats skimming with sails of flogged skin.
Inside a pelican's pouch he flies from island
to island, wreathing with rain-lilies
lighthouses, masts, and campanili.

In their shack of tamarind wood,
a chapel on stilts, the smoke of candles
vivifies fish heads (nailed to the wall)
to bleed, quiver, turn east at cock-crowing;
a procession of ants will then surrender
to the flames. Lye falls
from clouds of ash. Lenten night:
the resurrection ferns will again be lush

and green. Yesterday the sea was vinegary,
less brackish than customary for baptism.

Waves release rosaries gnarled
with bladder wrack that village youths
unravel to mourn another acolyte.
Fragrant as sweet plantain, three mulattas—
fishnet menders—sing a dirge in Lucumí,
pantomime the hammerhead's thrust
and thrash to sign the boy's martyrdom.

Yemayá, Lady of the Sea, spawned
without sin, light from darkest water,
spare the fisher's son, swaddle him with fish
guts, brood him under your manta wings.
That blinding aureole will forever
burn above your shark's-jaw crown.

The Tropics Reclaim Calvary

Passionflower vines
on banks of Yumurí
three royal palms
crowning a green hill
the central one
spires into a rainbow

In their allamanda bower
Sts. Lazarus and Barbara
drink rose-apple cider
eat avocado and turtle fricassee
rivulets of passion juice
cascade into gaping seraphim

Toes tapping bongos
Lázaro strums his crutch
with leprous fingers
lamenting his infirmities
"woe begets woe begets woe
I loathe rubbing urine
and tobacco on my boils"

Barbarita replies
warbling a *danzón*
to the sacred heart
"I died for you, no regrets,
mi cielo, mi gloria . . ."
her long cinnamon hair
ablaze with torch lilies

Lázaro feels jealous
toward Jesús—darkly

handsome—whom she's
loved for millennia

Lázaro's bones ache
as never before, wishes he were
an African god—beautiful,
healthy—who drums
the world enrapturing mortals
and immortals alike

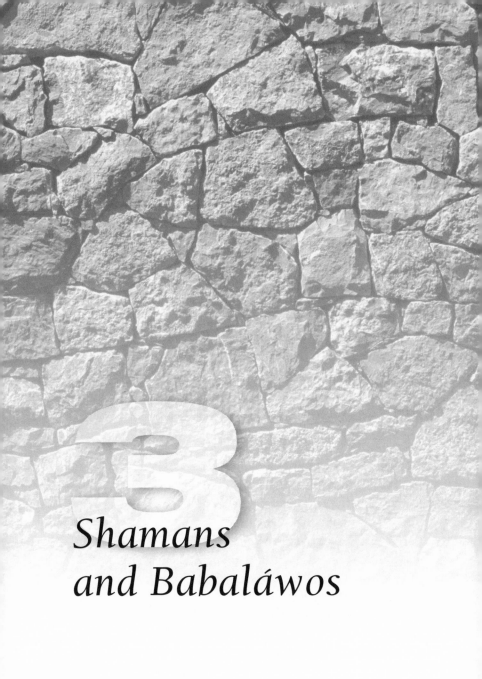

3

Shamans
and Babaláwos

Maurice Kilwein Guevara

A City Prophet Talks to God
on the 56C to Hazelwood

I say
Seems like everyone's sleepy as the Chessie cat
I say Captain
look at your river old Monongahela
Even John the Baptist would not wade in that water
Never mind I know the catfish big as sharks
Hmm mm Hmm mm
And the things they pull up from there
the bones of horses the bodies of men
grand pianos pig iron toilets Singer sewing machines
two railroad ties crossed
spiked at the breastbone
old cars even parking meters down there time expired

God
don't be like the people tell their children sit far away
like the man from the State says Take your pill Take your pill
Don't talk back cause you might alarm the other passengers
But he says I know you know they know
they're just puppet voices in your head
You think my brain's polluted with intergalactic debris
I think we're all lice on a fat rat's back
rolling down the incline
into the river of the Anti-World
Smile
while the orphan child dresses us for the wake
Wake
and suffer the wildflowers to come unto me
Hazelwood Avenue
Ring the bell Ring the bell

I say
Even the Turk's-cap of God will rust in the Garden of Old Raw
   Iron
I say
This is my stop
This is where I step down

The Fifth of November

By morning Mass in Belencito, my mother claims, she
knew I would be born before noon. Her friend Inés put her
nose in my mother's scalp and disagreed. "When it's time the
roots of your hair will smell like *guayaba*." The priest was
lifting the silver vessel above his head. In that curved and
polished metal, the acolyte who would become a famous
painter saw the open legs of my mother at the exact moment
her water broke. A fox was whimpering outside the church
and everyone agrees it was very, very windy that morning.
My birth certificate states I was born with a harelip at five
minutes to noon.

My mother kept her white socks and black shoes on
during labor. I remember the explosion of light, foreign as
English or Spanish. To make this house, many of us were
crushed under pillars of wood.

Christ have mercy. Lamb of God. *Ite Missa est.*

Why Given to Be Adopted

for Diego and Andrés

I once saw the face of Mohammed's Fatima in a grain of wild rice.

The human brain has more cells than the universe has stars and I imagine a crib in which a blind infant opens her eyes and listens to the *this* and *that* of crickets. You *open* your mouth and *trago* makes you swallow. Four yellow handprints on a white piece of paper is my word for *brothers*.

Your first mother at the broken window has a firefly like the stone of a ring on her longest finger and watches it go away in the night. Faith and courage.

The unknowable is a wildcat who lives at the crest of the ridge. Feel lucky if you ever see her eyes reflecting starlight toward you. Once in a playground on the spinning world I felt her soft pant on my neck.

River Spirits

When animals were no longer people, I was walking with my young sons along the river of the sliding banks. Thick plugs of wild asparagus were pushing up through the earth, and in the darkness of the forest thousands of white flowers pricked our eyes like stars. My little one was kneeling in the mulch and pine brushes, pulling back the green vertebrae of a fern. Suddenly he called out. I thought perhaps he'd found fox scat or a white spider until we crouched beside him and saw the Monongahela village.

Dwellings stretched the length of a finger, wattled walls and matted roofs. Hunters in buckskin huddled around a stone, and we could smell the gray thread of burning tobacco. A line of waterfowl were flying north over the village, not far from the orange cooking fire. Under the widest part of the fern, the older children and five women were hunkering or bent in the garden, laughing and weeding around the goose-foot, the green pumpkins, the bright sunflowers taller than the old storytelling man drinking from a gourd.

"I am finished," he said, "it is the end."

Cofradía

How many times do I have to tell you Yes
I wear the black hood of a common saint
following stars and the smell of *basuco*
straight in my mission as the one bullet
cutting a way through the fifteen years
of your crazy skull   The moon
empties of her marrow in the dirt
I lay on you a dark rose whose stem
cannot hold the petals   Dead One
I walk away
leaving the three spirits
to do their work in peace
as I will do mine
Tomorrow is another night   O missionaries
we are brothers on the dark road

How many times do I have to tell you

Good Friday

Doomed as any bell, she lifts you in her arms again. You are flying over a small town in America. Black roofs like open match covers, people tiny as toys: one mails a letter, one bends over her laundry basket, and unseen, one cries and cries in his bed. Like wildflowers, there is a sprinkling of children on a green hillside. High, faraway laughter. And there lies the cemetery, gravestones like crooked teeth. Look: a farmer rides down Main Street on a yellow tractor. A woman on the sidewalk waves to him. He waves back. The wind is peaceful that carries the gulls. Brown fields are everywhere waiting for seed. The town is happy to be alive.

She is your bride, this woman holding you in her arms. You hear her breathing. And the soft beating of her heart. Finally she lowers you to earth, at the crossing of two side streets, whispering: "Christ could be anyone. Anything." Then she hands you an orange, and it burns bright in your palm like the sun.

I Sing on the Day of the Deceased

in memory of José Asunción Silva

> . . . sube a nacer conmigo, hermano.
> —Neftalí Reyes

I

Campesinos and green-tailed birds eat gladly from the
    strawberries
and morning glories twisting
up the trellis of my spine
I play turtleback guitar   ghost flute   conch
I am nothing but bone and American song

II

I am zero

I am dogwood flowering pink

I am the little howls of Chiapas

I am the moan in the *caracol* at Guayaquil

I sing against the National Police who violated her small body

I cup my hands over my skull to hear stars

I am the catch in the throat of Quechua

I am the baby shepherd in a pen of *cuy*

I am the voice of corn and *yuca*

I am drums I am Changó *el gran putas*

I root into the wall of you

I am the wizened Aleut praying in the Russian Church

I know the world is wide and alien and emerald

I ride with Edchewe on the perilous journey to sun and moon

III

I am your brother   lover   sister   *bisabuelo*
                                        these bones
Eat from my vines the rubies the funnels of blue
Listen to the sound of rain on stone
The flute I blow
was once that happy arm that held you in the dark

Adrián Castro

Cancioncita pa la Ceiba/Song for the Sacred Mother Tree

The ancient Lukumí
swimming in clouds of cotton
used to say
Eluayé ni mo se o Eluayé mi baba
Eluayé ni mo se o Eluayé mi baba
Obatalá ta wi ni wi ni se kuré
Araba iya

When the gentle trade winds
speak
when they consult the ceiba tree
on matters beyond their perceptions
she responds by twirling her leaves
like an alchemist does to dust from the heavens
she responds by directing her branches
as a Taíno did to fish
towards the crossroads where
symbols that hold the key
to tomorrow's tears
or yesterday's fiesta
are about to arrive
on the wing of a wind
or the gust of a hawk

The ancient Lukumí used to say
when clouds were swimming in cotton
Eluayé ni mo se o Eluayé mi baba
Obatalá to wi ni wi ni se kuré

Araba iya
In African jungles she was teak
but when her children were
kidnapped
they could not bring her
aboard
ships whose wood squeaked the word
torture
so her children captured her strength
captured her power
& disguised it in the steel that bound them
the steel that killed them
She assumed a new identity
on her trip to a region
where mangos walk hand in hand
with guanábanas
& bananas relax on street corners
A region which an exaggerated breeze
brisa exagerada
named Hurakán
visits every summer & pens
a manifesto of destruction
Her name is now Silkcotton
that is
ceiba
Madre Ceiba
& Hurakán dares not
carve its name on her trunk

The ancient Lukumí used to say
when cotton was swimming in clouds
Eluayé ni mo se o Eluayé mi baba
Araba iya
as they circled the steps
engraved by ancestors shook-shaking
campesinos communing with

chanting to
Mamita Ceiba
'round midnight
Those who in Matanzas
buried in her feet
cocos tattooed with tribal symbols
words wrapped in a banana leaf
to inject them with magic
necklaces/elekes
bathed in riverwater
seawater
tabaco ash—
amulets against broken
rhythm

Here the air is pregnant with droplets—
water drops in
unannounced
we are all expectant mothers
waiting for the air to burst
So we ask Mamita Ceiba
to shelter us from
heaven's tears
as we watch the years
in a lake
dance like a holy wave
a deeper shade
of cha-cha-cha—
the dance that put the lid on the jar
the dance like her leaf
the dance like her branch—

saludos a la Madre Ceiba
Araba iya o

Para la Installation de José Bedia

Que tus son Kongo
emi ni son Yoruba
canto en inglés—

The marriage of spirit & history
is often like a dance of streams
dance of rainbows
like sending smoke signals yes there is
                hope
& yes we can resist the urge to forget

The brick boat
with its shadow about to speak
tells the story
So we gather bits of myth—
something like balsas
something like torn cloth
armed with little war instruments
Shovel & hoe to erect roots
(they can be amuletos so long you keep them in yr pocket
   necklace yr head)
Something like rope
like white head tie
to provoke stability & peace of mind
Something like strewn slipper de niño
we call this chancleta
we call this sorrow

Que tu son Kongo
emi ni son Yoruba
canto en español—

E yo hala garabato mi Kongo
mi Kongo

Kongo real
hala garabato halo

We who are born from river water
sea water
tambor y trueno
repique de brisas & stones
We who circle clouds of cotton
with a certain chant
We who choose el canto—
in Spanish or Kongo Biriyumba
Osha Lukumí
Monina Nkamá
in Arará kwero Dahomey e e
We who build shrine to migration
We who die with
river water sea water
tambor y trueno
repique de brisas & stones

Those who cast the first balsa
in the bombardment of boats
who cast a desperate wail
Pablo, Antonio, Miguel
maybe even Raquel
They said one throws the rock
but it's the people who get blamed
it's the people who get blamed
when one throws the rock
(*Oye basta de cuento*
llegó el momento de—)
Those who cast the first balsa
even though they've seen empty
even bitten inner tubes
lying softly on a breezy shore
even though they seen the iron rudder
with the signature of Sarabanda Kimbansa

strewn on a pile of stones
strewn like dead fish

He who struts con crutches
but dances without them
has a body of trembles
but inside has signs of infinity—
a dog can be his messenger

San Lao San Lao
Kobayende San Lao

He who sits at crossroads
changing destinies with a funny dance
sometimes from pebble to sugar
from sugar to pebble

Que tu son Kongo
emi ni son Yoruba
canto en Lukumí—

Eshu odara ibá re o
Orúnmila kò sóro odá ni òfò
kò sóro òfò ni odá
Ifa rí o
Adashé
Four twins spin a hymn—
something about opening yr eyes
to what is before you
(Irósun meyi)
about being led into a trap
(Irósun meyi)
They said no one knows what's at the bottom of the sea
They said you must be careful
There's someone with big boots
standing on a shore
& yes there's a hole just ahead
You must be careful
the ocean seems to be hungry these days—

76

The Mysteries Come to the Bridge

for Edouard Duval Carrié

The mysteries come to the bridge
The embarkation can be Haitian
      itself a basket of fruits
      forced to float from Ibo, Yoruba, Kongo
            Dahomey country
The embarkation can be Cuban too
      itself a canasta of fruits
      the mysteries come al son
            de tambores batá

There are fish who kiss this boat
they too are wise because they witness & remember
Ochún quien es Ezuli
Ogún es Ogu (aquí viene Ogún, Ogún, Ogún)
Loko es Iróko
      Iróko/Loko (ko ko ko)
Legba/Elegba, Eshu Odara
      who delivers messages with a morse code of offerings
Dambala coiled in a snake of white cloth
          Obatalá y/o Nana Burukú

Yemajá/Olókun
         Olókun/Agwe
hosting the onslaught of oars
on their soft tablecloth of blue
Orúnmila slowly sang the journey—Ifá

They departed like a whispered incantation
        the shore was assisted by
           sea grapes which we call uva de caleta
           by lengua de vaca
           by albahaca
And there were crabs y carey
who tore only an antenna

only an eye
while the other bid farewell
It was quiet

This story is repetitious
Their boat was made of calabash—
        they sliced the upper world & this world
        they used the upper to cover their heads
        the lower to dance on water
        There were certain signatures
            incantations etched
        there were smaller gourds dangling on the sides
            some beaded some painted
        History has it they were packed with juju
            the ancestor of mojo
            le dicen brujería
            le dicen nishé Osayin

When the embarkation arrived
    smooth like fingers sliding through powder
they saw a similar scene
The flora smiled
        like an old friend:
    Botón de oro spilled a golden button
    Peregún with its bayoneta provided defense
    Campanas rung their silent scent
    And there was Ceiba
        Iróko's brother who they called
                Araba
        —it too had a white cloth circling its trunk—
The mysteries smiled
    Tradition migrated

When the embarkation arrived
only the names had changed
names changed
like yours
like mine

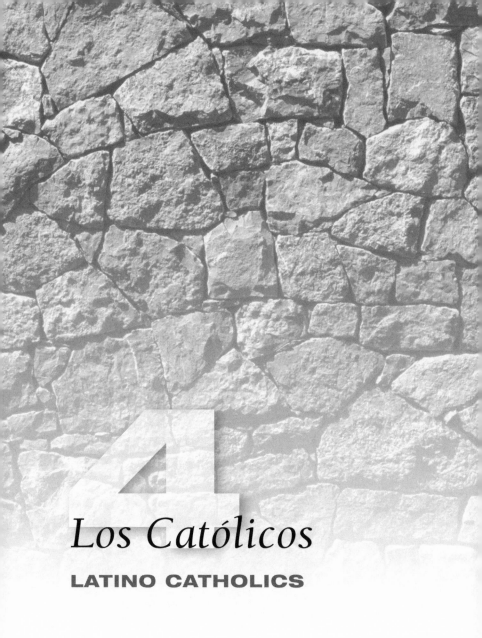

4

Los Católicos

LATINO CATHOLICS

Benjamín Alire Sáenz

Crucifix

Palo Alto, California
Summer, 1988

It shone like a still sea in the stove-burner sunlight
of the Western drought. (A long drought that year
and I in the middle of it. Water everywhere in my dreams.)

It shone, a luminous stone, smooth, hard
but—to my eyes—silky, soft as skin, tender leaves
on spring trees, touched by rain. Light green pigments

mixing with pinks of early summer roses—growing
against the dull dawns, the dusty straw-yellow skies.
A garden—a sea—to be lost in. Mirage—was just

a piece of dirt, soft clay baked into hardness
created from the dust. Just an object, man-made.
It should have been enough to touch the smooth

curves which rolled like valleys and hills on its
earthen surface. It should have been enough—why
possess the clay? I took it home, placed it on a

nail in the wall. It hung like a crucifix, secure,
and though the drought continued (day and night, unbroken
chain of heat, endless calendar of dust) my thirst

subsided. When I moved, I packed my ceramic
with care, with rare patience, convinced it was protected
from all harm. When my belongings arrived in my new

home, I opened the well-taped box with my name
written on all its sides and found my ceramic in
pieces. Broken in transit. Baked earth cracks

and is lost. I picked the sharp-edged pieces from the box
like a farmer examining a harvest, surveying the season
of loss. Unable to accept the brokenness which had arrived

at my door, I began to place each fragment on the floor
until I had formed from the memory the piece I purchased.
I began to glue it slowly. Hour after hour, I worked,

moved to save. I knelt on the floor—lost
in the labor like a novice begging for faith, the water
of his hurt gone dry: "Come back, come back . . ."

Alone, I lived in the silence of re-creation
until I brought it back to life. It hangs now
an awkward, crooked ceramic, a wide-cracked

sculpture that screams of an original smoothness. In its
shattered state, it is something beyond the work of its maker.
I stare at it daily, memorize the cracks, reminders of drought

and water. It hangs in my house, a crucifix of brokenness,
of fragile resurrection. It hangs—tenuously—never again
secure. Any day, it will fall from its place or again be

shattered in the movements of life. I will kneel, re-glue it,
transform it once again. It will hang forever on my wall.

Cemetery

Mesilla, New Mexico
Day of the Dead, 1988

    I walk these grassless grounds
Cracked, withering in weeds. My eyes move
From one monument to the next: a star
For the hour of their births, a cross
For the hour of their deaths. Grave after
Grave, row after crooked row like fields
Of rotting corn.
            My eyes fall
On words: *Para mi querido hijo,* a mother's
Final letter to her war-dead son. The foreigner
Has found a place, died for a flag that knows only
How to wave *adiós* in English. A broken angel,
Wingless, protects the grave of an infant
Whose name the wind has stolen.
                A cloud
Covers the sun. It will not rain. I stand
In this noonday darkness somewhere between
A cross and a star, strip off my clothes, rags
That hide my bones. Bones. Bones fighting to bare
Their blankness to open air. I strip, listen
To the sound of my skin scrape against the earth,
And dance to the music of the only instrument
I ever learned to play: the dirt. The silent,
Too silent, biographer, the earth. The earth.

Sacrifices

Mesilla Park, New Mexico
May, 1962

We are in the center, my brother and I. Our hair
Cut so short, it stands straight. Shiny, it glitters,
Catches light. *If only they had let us*
Grow our hair long.
                              On this late spring Sunday, we pose
Holding candles, black prayer books, plastic rosaries. Ribbons
tied to right arms, white and swaying like large leaves
Wanting to tear free of the tree. *If only there was life*
Without the tree. Our white shirts, new, respectfully worn;
Our black pants pressed with perfect lines from Mama's iron.
Our clothes stiff; we yearn to strip. Today,
We must endure them.
                              Our smiles restrained. Having eaten
Of the bread, partaken of the sacrifice we witnessed on the altar,
Adults now. We saw. We took. We ate. Adults, having tasted
The Catholic God. Our tongues still tingling from the touch
Of the white host. Today we are good. Today, we take our place,
   follow
The path that has been worn down by the generations before us
To make our travels lighter. *If only we could walk*
Another road. Today, we step.
Safe.
         Pushing and pulling, our grandmothers behind us:
Tall statues with thinning hair. Skin already eroded
By their many rituals of sacrifice. Statues no longer worshipped
By men, but perfect for boyhood love. Their hands
On our shoulders pushing us down towards earth, pulling us
Up towards sky. We, newly harvested corn,
Perfect offerings for their hungry God.

Easter

Mesilla, New Mexico
Spring, 1962

My mother woke us that Sunday—her voice
a bell proclaiming spring. We rose
diving into our clothes, newly bought.
We took turns standing before mirrors,
combing, staring at our new selves.
Sinless from forty days of desert,
sinless from good confessions, we
drove to church in a red pickup, bright
and red and waxed for the special
occasion. Clean, polished as apples,
the yellow-dressed girls in front
with Mom and Dad; the boys in back,
our hair blowing free in the warming
wind. Winter gone away. At Mass,
the choir singing loud: ragged
notes from ragged angels' voices;
ancient hymns sung in crooked Latin.
The priest, white-robed, raised his palms
toward God, opened his mouth in awe:
"Alleluia!" The unspoken word of Lent
let loose in flight. Alleluia and incense
rising, my mother wiping her tears
from words she'd heard; my brother and I
whispering names of statues lining
the walls of the church. Bells ringing,
Mass ending, we running to the truck,
shiny as shoes going dancing. Dad
driving us to see my grandmother. There,
at her house, I asked about the new word
I'd heard: *resurrection.* "Death,

death," she said, her hands moving downward, "the cross—*that* is death." And then she laughed: "The dead will rise." Her upturned palms moved skyward as she spoke. "The dead will rise." She moved her hands toward me, wrapped my face with touches, and laughed again. *The dead will rise.*

Clay Woman Holding Her Sacred Heart

To Karen (who already knows)

Nun? Saint? Penitent whore? Devoted follower of The Little Flower
Of Jesus or reincarnation of Hester Prynne? Other clay figures
   around her,
But they—they wear yellow and pink robes of spring, hold
            candles, flowers,
Children in their arms, hands closed tight around the treasures
   they adore.
Strong as they are, what they hold fast with their arms
               must someday be
Unloosed, but not today. She stands near those created by the same
Hands, the same clay, yet she lives separate. In her Lenten
         garments she stands
Solitary—in a strange exile. She is of the earth, nothing more than dirt,
But
                  She has been elected by her maker to be a beacon
In the night, to fight, to suffer with her devils and her God. She
   walks in
Darkness, walks in light—withstands the loneliness of life. She holds
Open her palms. She is holding a thing bigger than her hands—awful
And red as the winter sun sinking into a cold cold sea. It is a heart
She holds, the heaviest of burdens. The heart is wet with blood. She was
Molded, baked, painted in Mexico where any saint worth
         praying to must be
Adorned with blood as well as gold. Among the poor, blood's the
   proof
Of faith. One pays for holiness with flesh.
                           In El Norte, we like our icons
Bloodless. We believe in woundless resurrections. We like
   our tombs empty
And well-swept. In the North—where we live—the poor
   have no advantage:
Blessed be the poor—and blessed be the rich for they are poor in spirit.

The Kingdom of God is lovely and conveniently democratic.
        Unless a grain
Of wheat falls to the earth and dies, it remains alone; but if it dies,
It bears much fruit. Let us not speak of the price. Let us not
Speak of the heart that must be ripped from its safe,
        protected place.
                        She holds
This bloody heart as if it were the largest jewel on earth.
She exhibits her breakable stone, the place where sorrows begin—
Sorrows that have stained her hands and garb with indelible marks
Of pain. She cannot wash that source of torment in the world.
        She will not
Hide the visible sign that makes her use her hands—the sign that
    forces
Her to touch: hands steady, she holds out her only offering. Older
    now,
She has learned her own secrets. She has cast out the shame of her
    past.
She no longer has need of her pride. She is no longer afraid to
    surrender
Her last possession. It has been given many times. She has felt its
Absence, wept each time she has lost it: each time growing accustomed
To the lifelessness of losing it, each time embracing the numbness
Of nothingness. But always the heart returned beating strong as
    the wings
Of a young eagle in first flight.
                        Look closely at her face. See,
She is not in mourning. Her days of weeping are behind. *This is*
    her day
Of freedom. Palms open, she offers her sacred heart . . . *Unless a*
    grain
Of wheat . . .   Sins, she has many, but she can't repent
From the giving. There is peace in public stigmata . . . *but if it dies,*

A hundred wheatfields for the poor,

        a million loaves of bread for those who want.

The Adoration of the Infant Jesus

for Rose

> Nostalgia, from
> nostos: a return home; and
> algos: to be in pain

> After Mass this Christmas Day
> The people file out. This is
> All? Where are the lines?
> Expectant crowds? The clamoring
> Children waiting to kiss His feet?

I am standing with my mother, my father, my brothers,
And my sisters. I am standing on the tips of my toes
Stretching to see above the heads of those in front.
We crowd into the aisles, shove and push. I smell
Work and perfume; I smell starch and a woman's iron
On the immaculate clothes of those who stand and wait.
We stand together. Here, I am safer—protected in the warmth
Of Spanish. God is so in love with us. I can't wait
To see him. To kiss him, to kiss him. When my lips reach
His feet, he will turn to flesh. I know this. He will
Turn softer than silk, warm as a summer's night,
And he will smile at me. When I reach the holy place,
I stare at the priest who holds the Savior in his arms,
The altar boy who wipes His feet after every kiss.
The priest nods, and when my lips touch the child I have
Waited for, he is warm with the kisses of the people.
I feel the pulse of his blood running through the softness
Of his feet. I know he is breathing. He is alive. He
Is ours. The priest does not know what he holds,
But we who have kissed him know that he is real.

The people here
Do not believe
In lines. Some of us
Do not walk out
The doors. We cannot
Leave this church.
We are few, but we are
Sober as the morning winter
Light. Slowly, one by one,
We kneel before the scene:
A mother, a father, a son;
The sheep, and kings, an angel.
We have known them all our lives.
Mary, the Virgin, the Mother;
Joseph, the Worker, the Father.
The child, the Lover of flesh.
We will love them all our lives.

To the Desert

I came to you one rainless August night.
You taught me how to live without the rain.
You are thirst and thirst is all I know.
You are sand, wind, sun, and burning sky,
The hottest blue. You blow a breeze and brand
Your breath into my mouth. You reach—then *bend*
Your force, to break, blow, burn, and make me new.
You wrap your name tight around my ribs
And keep me warm. I was born for you.
Above, below, by you, by you surrounded.
I wake to you at dawn. Never break your
Knot. Reach, rise, blow, *Sálvame, mi dios,*
Trágame, mi tierra. Salva, traga, Break me,
I am bread. I will be the water for your thirst.

Prayer

for George

       The sky
is clear as gin.
I could lay my body
down, sleep in the calm
night, the peace of the winter
wind, and the deep black
sky that makes me forget
the morning light. Makes me
remember. Now I see
the stars, a million tongues
of fire. I am so
small. The earth beneath
my feet is giving, strong,
but slowly slowly
dying. Tonight
I want

      there has to be a God

The Wedding Feast at Cana

for Larry and Katy

*This, the first of his miracles, Jesus
performed at Cana in Galilee, and manifested his glory.*
—*John 2:11*

A man and woman meet. They fall
in love. This has been written; this
has been read; this is an old story.

In the body   there is a place:
those who work will know this space,
will know it's hard and holy, will
know it wears away the heart. We may
curse it day and night; we may
speak of it, point to it, pray to it—
it will not be appeased.

          Listen to your names:
their sounds are like
no other: whispers of the world
needing to know if there is joy.
Is there joy? Listen to the hunger
forever—that song will never cease.
The song is sad. *You
will never be full.* Stay. Listen
to the hunger. Do not turn
from that sound. You cannot
run from earth. *Naked
you came from the dirt. Naked you must
return.* Flesh is flesh and it is flesh
till death.

                      This day, words
like thirst, and flesh, and hunger
mean *marriage*. Water is turned
into wine. This is the day of miracles.
Take. Drink. The best has been
saved for the poor. Taste. This is the cup
of salvation. Be drunk. Touch. Make love
through the lonely night—but when you wake
remember: this wine is good and sweet
but you will thirst again.

The book of life is hard to write:
it is written with bone and blood;
it is written with hearts that labor
and labor, beat and beat until the walls
fall down. Begin. Write: in the kingdom
of the naked, working heart
shame is banished. A man and woman
meet—this is an *old—write it!*
Begin. Begin. Begin.

Miracle in the Garden

"I have seen the Lord."
      —John 20:18

You gave and gave, but it was not enough.
And there you were again—alone.
Another loss. Another wound. Another
scar: on the skin, in the heart, on the face.
The body wears the pain. Those hurts
come back—again—those hurts—again—
childhood and old lovers come back
always: they rise like Lazarus
needing no Jesus to command them back
to life. Overcome with grief—
more tears? So many droughts
and still more water in the well?
I sat across from you—in your garden—Spring—
and the sun shining like a new flower in bloom
haloing   you   me   the entire garden. You
did not notice the warmth. I was silent
in the presence of your grief. I was
there to pay respects, but not to speak.
In the sunlight, as I watched,
I had the urge to dip my hand
in the water of your tears,
and pray and bless myself
in the name of all your pain.

For a time, you walked that bridge
between the present and the past, between
this world and the next—*would it be better there?*
Your eyes stared blank—far—you
wanted to go, no longer wanting to choose
life. You sobbed out your regrets,

shook and shook your head. You clenched
your jaw as if to say: *I'll never love again,*
I'll never love. You grew quiet
listening to your god, or to your heart,
or to the western sun lighting up
the earth—the sun that set and rose,
the ceaseless sun that never tired
of the job that it was given. You felt
its labor on your skin. You were warmed—and then you
laughed. I saw you rising then. I saw you rise.

Diana Rivera

Poetry of the Holy Water

comes like a chameleon, placed
mysteriously by larger hands
between leaves and colors in the tuft
of earth,
a holy chameleon
cleverly, gently placed
by God, as two
humans meet:
cell to cell,
eye to eye, that endless
channel of depth and gratitude,
that sacred process
of the macro in the micro—
water, love—
infinitesimal
pure reactions:
division, or static calmness
(our movements perhaps naturalized
in the single, ever-moving point of peace)
or to choose dis/ease,
the entering into the pits and maladies
of our endless sorrows
through our bodies which are
really our souls,
because really we are all,
those we are with,
all which we see—
by giving pain we feel pain,
by giving love we feel love—
in the smallest tear perhaps the cure,

the relief from the small poison,
as water is everywhere
where there is life—
with forgiveness
a holy seed
sprouts calmly.

Prayer

Angels, Come!
Enter my cells, my bones, my hormones, my thighs,
this fleshy bud of heart,
this wretched blind mind with all her frail blooms,
this storm-cabbaged soul, where there are no souls.

Pierce me! Spades and hooks,
pluck this forlorn mood,
yank the bitter outlook, the dark aneurysm
in my looming sky.

What matters now is the earthly angel
who comes mornings softly, speaking gentleness.
I will take anyone! Who touches me softly!
Any breathing self that whispers compassion!

Oh, deserted being, all my women call,
nearer, nearer, the blood cornucopia.
Who has given me
this dark, second self?

Did it start with Eve? Is "the curse" believable?
Did the wicked hand that plucked the first Me-fruit
pluck me too, half-branched?

The dark angels laughed. One for immortality!
But it was a lie.
Listen to my heart.

Healing

for Trishia

She gave me the simple metaphor: the butterfly.
It swerved in the folds of her large, blue wings,
iridescent, refracting the shiny
crystal innocence
of her glimmering oceanic colors.
It swooned in the sanctuary of phosphorescent blooms
gleaming sea-joys
to suddenly fall crushed over her broken wings.
Do butterflies have hearts?   Frail ones?
With one small breath he stopped her flight.

In slow motion
wings unfold,
her heart pumps blood into her threaded veins,
re-connecting—the spectrum of blues
coalescing as shimmering
small glass chips
surfacing from a dense black ocean.

The gleaming
radiates lovingness
as the looming, unseen hand
pours a strange light,
gently retrieving
the sparkling blues
brightening wounds—
a raindrop sea-joy.

Merging the living from the dead,
innocence remains half lost
but faith and acceptance
weave at the core of her receptacles for flying.

Flying low to the ground, but steady,
the Divine Physician,
who in the eternal pat conceived
from mud wholeness and joy
pours the healing graces
until we believe in love again.

Lady of Light

Sorrow pours as I mourn my lost marriage.
Immersed in my center of sadness I dive
underwater
into the floods
and the breeding rains.
For days my heart has been a constant song of loss
and remembrance.
Memories shine as incandescent fossils.

But the Lady of Light rises from the city of pearls
to remind me—
as you grieve
pray for the awareness of the moments of joy
you hold today,
do not plunge into the depths,
do not dive in constantly.
The Spirit of God does not appropriate depression,
and joy travels below the river of grief.

Pray for the awareness of that joy,
for the hymn that feeds your grieving bones.
Listen to the winds of the spirit.
Dive not the glimmers of joy that breathe in the silent ache.
Don't pray for joy, for it's already with you.

Remember the heart weaves fantasies,
it weaves the love that could have been,
the moments, dear, that came not often.

Living Again

Walking in the woods with you, oh soul,
the brush embroidered lies awake and breathing,
the buttercups once sleeping waken
to hear immortal leaves and soliloquies.
Oh forlorn age of pain now ceasing
yet flaring raw in yesterdays still lingering—
Once the impassioned love that reached the heights of cupped
    elm branches
now dwells locked inside my torrid heart cells.
In grief our hearts seem to recall the tender souls we knew
before our birth.

To live again, to live again
and leave the bruised, strained shadows—
the desert of our exiled joys and fortresses of sadness,
the cities of lost yearnings
and pain eternal,
for love that deep, carves thus a pain as deep
and deeper.

To live again, to tread the lofty earth-spheres
where hay and clumps of soil and grass crumble between
    fingers,
where deer settle to sleep among tall Siberian Irises,
where gossamer roses, redeemed as buds,
break open to their singing petals.

To live again
walking with you, oh soul, in my eternal gardens
breathing sheer air, anemone, the sweetened grass

walking again this bright immortal forest
where all is clear and pure and simple.

Luminous Moon

Ethereal spirits walk the earth, lay down
quietly over the coves of valleys—
lovers, with heads buried between folds and mountainlegs,
closely observing
the crease of an upper thigh.

Clouds swam from above
because they desired
to touch our earthen, mortal matter.
The half moon, lit behind,
turns mist into pure afterglow, haloed
rose and green. She guides my way as the angelic—
never ceasing her everlasting protection.
She murmurs, sacred and calm.

It's soothing to know our Eternal Mother
as this moon, never leaves,
the oceans stay within their basins,
the Universe keeps its order,
even in darkness freely offering
light as reflection.

It's soothing to hear
the wings of light envelop us,
to feel the infinite protection,
the incomprehensible
pulsing love of God
endless in the million light years
pathway of stars
where each soul is precious.
Only this love can satisfy
the longings of the soul.

Pat Mora

Saint Martin of Porres
San Martín de Porres

Can I sing you, Brother Martin,
saint whose hands know work, like mine?
Would that we could sit together,
tell our *cuentos*, sip some wine.

Soon I'll close the church till morning.
Please guide me walking home alone.
Not a safe place for a woman.
Justice this old world postpones.

Speaking to our sweeping rhythms,
let us plot for those in need.
Can't you scare these stubborn faithful,
with your powers intercede?

Bread you gave to those in hunger,
kindness to the child alone,
held the trembling hand that suffered,
kindness from a man disowned.

Is it true when you were sweeping,
cats and dogs would come to chat,
telepathically you'd answer,
query disbelieving rats?

Brother Broom, with just a handshake,
you could cure a soul in pain.
Oh, I wish that you could touch me,
make these old joints fresh again.

Would that you had time to teach me
bilocation, such a trick,
not that I deserve the honor
and pleading seems impolitic.

You liked flying and liked gardens,
so practice aerial delights.
Come see *rosas,* tulips, daisies.
Can't I whet your appetite?

Ay, that I had seen the shining,
from your oratorio,
in your habit, man so prayerful,
that your very self would glow.

How we come, the dark-skinned faithful,
comforted to see you here,
able to confide our sorrows
to a black man's willing ear.

Your *corrido* I must finish
for priests frown at such casual songs,
frowning is their special talent,
but still, protect them all night long.

Help me listen to my garden,
cease wrinkled judgments based on skin,
our colored sacks like bulbs or seeds
that hold our fragrant selves within.

Saint Rose of Lima
Santa Rosa de Lima

Your name blooms in our mouths, Rosita,
your stories too, the pink blossom
floating above your crib, your petaled
face, and at your death, your flesh perfume.

Why were you stubborn as a thorn?

We burrow into your legends sweet,
cringe at hints you peppered your cheeks,
dragged a cross around your parents' yard,
hacked your hair, punished your soft self.

In that yard, you built a hut, lived alone,
you, mosquitoes and spiders who'd pause
when you prayed, hoping to hear His words
again, "Rose of My Heart, be thou My spouse."

Why were you so stubborn?

You heard voices: Mary, her Child,
Saint Catherine. Did they speak *en español,*
a music vibrating in your bones
like cellos praising a sunset?

Over forty years I've strained to hear
one sound, a whispered YES or NO
from any of you, my holy family.
Your silence tests my faith, dear friends.

Why are you so stubborn?

Tell me, Rosita, what is holiness?
Is it the ecstasy of sacrifice,
the body chained, whipped, punctured, deprived
of even hard bread and the shelter of sleep?

I know you wished to suffer like Our Lord,
but we women bleed enough, Rosita.
The body isn't evil, just heavy,
flesh unaccustomed to flight.

Why were you stubborn as a thorn?

Let me bring you down to smell these roses
from my garden. I tell them about you.
Like children, they like a story. Please
soften me into a garden of light.

Saint Francis of Assisi
San Francisco de Asís

Brother Sun, a warm greeting.
Wind sings green. I bring armfuls
of flowers, joy, such colors rising
to grace this day of pet blessings.

To grace this day of pet blessings,
and honor you, Brother Francis,
who heard the music of the earth,
song gathered and sent fluttering.

Song gathered and sent fluttering
into laughter, shouts, children parading
their dogs, lizards, cats, birds, toads, mice,
a lively line of squirmings.

A lively line of squirmings.
Manito, remember the worm,
the boy extending his palm,
his poverty confirming?

His poverty confirming,
with Brother Worm teaching me praise,
to listen to goats, donkeys, quail,
even fish, life's song affirming.

Even fish, life's song affirming,
so why, with all this gray hair
do I frown at muddy children, pets?
Your Carmen pokey at learning.

Your Carmen pokey at learning,
and yet I know you kissed lepers,
pressed yourself into what you feared,
transformed by your holy yearning.

Transformed by your holy yearning,
rolling in snow, on thorns to still
your body, Brother Ass, while I
stuff myself, to old sins returning.

Stuff myself, to old sins returning
like talking when there's work to do.
Sweet and sour children will soon stream
to my stern nose upturning.

To my stern nose upturning
while you hear their interior
light, flickering hum of the life-wick
within our fragile skin, glowing.

Within our fragile skin, glowing,
Christ's wounds on your flesh streaming
light, but had you come, ragged here,
I fear you'd see Carmen frowning.

I fear you'd see Carmen frowning.
Would I have stopped those pelting you?
Why can't I risk myself?
My silly pride's unsound.

My silly pride's unsound
while you softened a wolf
your words like keys freeing him,
his gentleness unbound.

His gentleness unbound.
Ah. How you would place your worn hands
on all we bring—turtles, roosters, hens.
You'd pray, each life affirming.

You'd pray, each life affirming,
me? Deceived by surfaces while larks
knew your spark, sang their morning song,
the evening your heart ceased burning.

The evening your heart ceased burning
yet those last years unable to see
but seeing the flame even
within Sister Pebble, blazing.

Within Sister Pebble, blazing
your eyes danced with each candle flame
you'd not bruise with your breath.
Teach me such attentive gazing.

Teach me such attentive gazing
before the squirming children come,
I raise my arms to Brother Sun
and pray to learn the joy of praising.

Demetria Martínez

Psalm

Damn the brain's chemical spills, evacuating
Every thought. Damn the smiles I pinned
To my face like a politician, a face
Like coffee with too much cream
Because I could not draw the
Curtain strings, raise the
Flag of a new day.
Weep, too, for the lost nights,
The poems, unfinished, because I locked
The canvas of my heart in a man's closet
And talked my way into his bed, instead.

God, do you remember? I was nineteen when
I saw the light of you escape like steam
From every living thing.
Now doctors say it was just
A tap dance of neurotransmitters.
But I know what I saw, how I heard your heart
In the heart of the Sandia mountains pump like an accordion.

You alone know I took notes, you alone
Know I wrote pages and pages
Of psalms.
And lost them on the road
Down a red-ribbed mesa north of Albuquerque.

Twenty years later I am rewriting them,
Remembering, dismembering.
God, will you forgive me if I call them poems?

Virgil Suárez

The Nuns in the Family

Here's my disclaimer: I don't know the first
thing about religion and I'm not religious.
My mother doesn't know this about me,
she likes to believe I still believe, still prays
to Saint Jude for my well being. Whenever
the subject of religion comes up, I excuse
myself and go to the bathroom or pick up
a magazine. See, I don't want to come out
and blame the two nuns in our family, who
visited us in Madrid when we lived there
(thanks to them, my mother says, we were
able to get out of Cuba) but the two weeks
they spent with us, they took me to church
with them twice a day, once in the morning
and once in the late afternoon, at a time
when the children (eleven, like me) were out
playing soccer in the park, and there I was
with these two perfect strangers, dressed
like *urracas,* walking to church. Two
weeks, and each visit they made me confess.
I confessed dry, made up stuff when I ran
out of the usual mischief I told the screen
in the confessional. The voice behind
the screen always said the same thing, pray,
pray for your sins. What sins? I thought.
Each time during mass, I felt awkward:
when people stood, I sat, when they knelt,
I stood. What travesty. Then one day,
glorious with sunshine, as we walked to church,
a truck full of bulls headed for the plaza

stopped and a bull jumped out of the back
and ran down the street, headed directly
toward us, and when the nuns started to pray,
a man pushed me out of the way into a shop.
The bull kept running toward us until a *Guardia*
Civil took out his gun and shot the bull
right in front of the nuns. The bull's legs
buckled under and the animal fell at their feet.
The nuns crossed themselves, grabbed my hand
and rushed me down the sidewalk toward church.
I told the story in the confessional and there was
more silence than usual coming from behind
the screen. A miracle said the voice finally.
Miracle? What miracle? I was confused
and I said so for which I was told to pray
more than ever before, in punishment.
The nuns never brought up the bull incident,
and after two weeks they left us for their convent
in Seville. So, these days when the nuns
in the family come up in conversation,
I start thinking about confessing stuff
I haven't even done, pure mischief,
like when I took off my big red T-shirt,
tapped on the door of the confessional,
and when the priest came out and put his fingers
up to his forehead to simulate the horns on a big
bad bull, I put the move of the matador on him,
shouting (and you could hear the echoes
inside the basilica): *Olé, toro, olé toro,* HA!

San Lázaro's Procession

It started at dusk or early that morning
in Havana (or was it dusk?) by the time
devotees moved through our neighborhood

many dressed in white, those on their knees
already bloody and scarred, others sunk
into their crutches, the absence of limb

obvious, pant leg folded and tucked
at the knee. All broken, damaged somehow
in this life, intent on kept promises. All

on their way to El Rincón de San Lázaro,
up on the hill, so far from where these people
had started their pilgrimages, to see

that old leper in loin cloth, surrounded
by his three faithful dogs which lick
and heal his festering wounds, the saint

the catholic church doesn't recognize,
says is only myth, but what about these
believers, moving through on pure will?

My parents brought me to the side of the street
where people in Calabazar stood
and watched the procession of the sick

and infirmed, not unlike the rest of us,
penitent of sins, expectant that a kept promise
could set them on the right path to freedom.

I was never taken to the place where they say
people left their offerings: casts, crutches,
hair, medicines for bad hearts, bad teeth,

flowers—left there at the altar by people
who claimed some certain healing took place
in their lives, and they merely walked away,

healed, new. I was a child in the awe
of such searches of spirit to a Cuban saint
whose charm I would never understand,

but so many, unlike me, so lifted by faith
and trust, moved by their beliefs, came through
so much hardship, determined in their passing—

bent on this idea left to them, they made
the journey to the little hilltop sanctuary
in the dark of their land, of my childhood.

So many people passed to leave some mark,
some token, like this poem, an amulet left
as a gift in the shrine of such yearning.

Clothespins / Los palitos de tendederas

In Sunday school we used them to make crucifixes.
      One clothespin at a time. We got them from the nun
who ran the school, in a shoe box marked with a cross,

      the smell of codfish on the pins, their metal springs
strewn like silver minnows between the cardboard
      and the wooden pieces. We used glue, beads, buttons;

mine had Christ sculpted with toothpicks and matches,
      a red button for a crown. The nun, Sister Nola,
liked my crucifix very much, said she liked suffering,

      then took me upstairs to see her Mother Superior.
We creaked up the dark and winding stairs, the ring
      on her hand tap-tapped as she gripped the shiny banister.

      I thought of my classmates still working on their crucifixes,
designing, gluing, placing their own ornaments. Sister Nola
      opened a door to a room, guided me inside, sat me down.

She walked away into another room. I sat and stared
      at the dusty, worn furniture. Everywhere the musty
brown of old age, sadness. Sister Nola spoke in a whisper

      to another person, and I thought of her mother, bed-
ridden, a sack of bones on a bed, as Sister Nola told us.
      I heard laughter, or was it coughing? The clearing of phlegm

in a throat. A rustling of curtains or clothes or a pulled rug.
      When Sister Nola returned, she was naked. She stood
in front of me. I saw her pale skin, the rivers of blue

      veins on her waxen breasts, the dark nipples. Suddenly,
I could have fainted, but I sat there and looked at her
      long enough to see a red halo form around her head.

I thought of the button I glued on as Christ's thorns
      on my crucifix. She held it in one hand, burning there,
a glow so bright I believed the sun had swallowed us both.

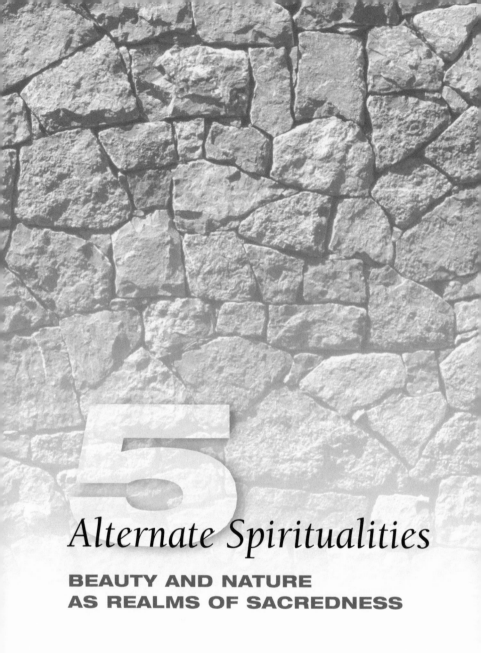

5

Alternate Spiritualities

BEAUTY AND NATURE AS REALMS OF SACREDNESS

Richard Blanco

Relativity

It's about perspective. The stars we see, see
us and all of life's little objects spinning
with the earth and hurling toward a void
somewhere near Lyra or Corona Borealis—
absolutely nothing is ever absolutely still:
not the bundle of gardenias slowly browning,
nor the photo frames of the dead and alive
wreathed with leather-white petals seeming
so incapable of anything on their own.
Not the wool sweaters in the summer closet,
nor old birthday cards, tickets, and matches
forgotten in a drawer of remember whens.
Not the upside crystal nor the cloistered china;
not the bouquet of pens in the coffee can,
nor books like granite strata on the desk,
nor the desk, nor the furniture no one sits on.
Not the arms vined around pillows and bodies
held in a dark room by gravity or the gravity
of living, so convincing this perfect stillness
of wreckage orbiting steadily around the sun.

It's about light. Stars are a memory of light
burned out billions of years ago—look—
they may not be there, it's more frightening
than the gaps of darkness between them.
In light of this, darkness is sweeter sometimes,
so much easier to click the lamp off, fold
a page, shut the book, set a cheek against
an arm that is not a vine but flesh, and sleep
when the mind has lost its armor of reason,
when the body lies prayerless and unveiled,
in a room the size of a life. Easier to love
the dead to write letters never to be sent,
to waste gardenias before they lose their scent,
to live out of a drawer stuffed with the past
rather than to turn the crystal over and drink
cheap wine or pink champagne and, hell,
smash the plates into irreconcilable pieces,
reach for the speed of light, accelerate
and warp the mind a little mile after mile
per second per second per ever per ever.

Morning on the Shore

after the storm
the covenant   driftwood returning like names
of debris   of things I thought I had
                the still innocence   forgotten
                of each rounded stone
                willing to wait
the sea's offerings   the eternity I cannot
rusting alive
in their own salt   gossamer blue veils
                of man-o-wars
                as irresistible as they are
                untouchable

      hardened pieces of red
      coral like wishbones   broken over wishes
                                        I've wished and
                                          wished again,
over rain-starched sands
that take no footprint   the silvery bodies
                      of tiny fish flickering
                      on the shore a few at a time
                                      reclaimed by the ebb
                                          of each wave
a filmy bottle, a torn net, a buoy
at the end of a snapped fishline
a dead fish, eyes bulged   heaps of washed-up sea grass
                            anonymous and spent

                  I know:

the flat-yellow bulldozer will rake the shore,
leave a scar of tire tracks, a ghost of diesel smoke
    like an offering of noxious incense to the heavens
           in the name of the nameless vanishing

vanished by mid-morning——
   I have work to do, words——
          to find and fix
             a life

Dionisio Martínez

Ash Wednesday

When Michelangelo created man, he was anticipating cracks all along the ceiling. With the years and the wars to come, he expected at least this much. The same theory that split the continents made room for this man looking down from the ceiling to pull away from God, to pull away long enough to think a while. He hasn't made up his mind yet. Michelangelo also thought that the inability to make up one's mind is—in some strange way, with some distorted logic—a kind of decision. Michelangelo's man is drawing closer to this concave God if you buy the continental drift theory: all movement away from something is movement *toward* something. It is quite conceivable that the paint will fall before the roof caves in, doing away with the universe across the ceiling. It is not likely, but it is possible to find under all the dust and the flakes of paint the two hands finally touching—the man's forefinger and God's forefinger resting on each other on the floor of the basilica. My instincts promise me another God: a convex figure, something that is constantly expanding like a bubble, moving toward me. I am lying on the dome of the basilica. Michelangelo's universe has been painted on the outside. I am crawling up to the two fingers that will not meet. I am going to resolve everything. There will be nothing to talk about once I accomplish my distortion of history. There will be nothing left for the critics, no lines to read between, no distances for the amateurs to interpret. But the theory holds true here too: once you make the two hands touch, you sever the arms from their bodies. I face the dilemma of doing nothing or making historians write about Michelangelo's one-armed God and his one-armed man and how the two suffer from a common delusion. They say that when a limb is cut off, one still feels it on the body. The one-armed creations on the dome are imagining their missing limbs intact. They can keep trying to touch, but sooner or later they must give in to the gravity of their convex universe. I have not changed the outcome of things. I have only altered the manner in which the two figures try to rise from the dust of their separate histories.

Valerie Martínez

Tesoro

for Timothy Trujillo
*   1951-1991*

Just a few years ago, when everything was permanent.
Or on the edge of. Or, yes, perhaps over the edge,
or falling away from—

Was like the façades of the Sagrada Familia
with their delicate foliage, swans and turtles
bearing the weight of. Everything alive
& carved out of stone.

It was my treasure, this permanence,
the architecture of living. Everything
stone-true & buttressed: arc & arc & arc
of an ancient city.

Can you guess what will come next? Can you?
Touching you like the sheerest handkerchief
of silk? When the beloveds fell from the sky
& disappeared? From stone to diaphanous silk.
On the wind. Sudden.

It was a mistake, amiss. It was perception,
of what is light as what is heavy & permanent.
Sometimes, one's hand can pass though stone,
& it is not a dream.

One got sick & another, another.
Someone I loved, who loved me,

disappeared. Two, or is it three,
who died. This is honest enough,
enough to say bluntly.
This is for Tim.

In *The Visitation* it is beautiful:
the handmaid's arms are barely covered,
tender skin beneath transparent silk.
The painter made no mistake,
the maiden is the most present of all.
She could be taken on the wind
with those invisible wings
& she is real, impermanent.
Her weight compares to no universe.

To hear it in my sleep—*tesoro*—
the hardest gift I'll come to accept.
In the cities of dreams my delicate arms
reach out toward the substantial,
to the place where they've all gone.
Goodbye.
Everything is like thin paper here.
Sometime, I'll see you all there.

The Annunciation

after the painting by Martini & Lemmi, quattrocento

It has been, and always will be
the way she leans back,
pulls her blue robe under her chin.
There is a golden shadow behind her:
halo, echo of another robe,
like a form she is about to take on.
She is the mother of Christ;
her book is closing upon her thumb.
It is hard for her to listen.

In the same way we are hesitant.
Delegations meet with the prospect
of peace but in separate rooms,
like couples with interminable
distances. They do not fear
the other's death like the lover
who waits for the next irregular breath
of she whom he loves. I am speaking,
for all I know, of listening.

Gabriel, on the left side of the painting,
utters his announcement.
Breath and sound become matter—
gold letters cross the panel:
room . . . atmosphere . . . lilies . . .
to the one who pulls away.

It is of course imaginable, predictable.
How is it possible for her to believe?
The ambassadors are witnesses
to a slide show, given everything
from the intricate filagrees of moss

to the round eyes of starving children,
from sea life to exploding stars.
It was obvious, the impossible
so real and obvious that this planet
and their allegiances, well,

I am out of breath.
Will breath become gold?
(And Mary will think *yes*.)
Will it move across.
(She will lean forward and dream *yes*.)
Something is trying to tell us,
waiting for us to take on
the brilliant shadow.
And if we would listen
(believing and saying *yes*)
who knows how the message
would become matter
then manifest itself.

Heat of Breath

"Ancient Semites taught that the sacrum
at the base of the spine contained a mystical
seed of each person's future resurrected body."
                    The Women's Dictionary
                    of Symbols and Sacred Objects

And so, at the end, the cloud
    which takes the shape
of neck, torso, and foot,
    exhaled from a mouth
in the back, is a cloak,
    somehow familiar.

What will the body be there?
    Mirror-Image? Hush
of the Past? Who planted
    this seed, fed by flesh,
speaking its name
    from first light to darkness.

Whose mouth blows into it
    with love, loverly,
heat of breath, and so,
    who makes us?

O Story of Influence

The hurricane's void eye. The pinwheel
furiously rolling across. The weatherman's
grinning fascination. The winds—so many
miles per hour, so many islands per day.
Where it will sweep, stop, smash into.

> Out of the center
> is the child, half-formed,
> face blooming. Eyes
> and eye. The shroud,
> her gauzy visage.

> Mouthing four words.
> We don't know them.
> There, hovering.

How many dead. The most rural places
inaccessible. This man wailing in the debris.
These hills of mud sliding, houses these
matchsticks flowing by. Our televisions
flashing. Our gazes transfixed.

> There she is. Still. Across
> the diameter of the storm.
> Across, across.

> Her feet stuck in the spin.
> Beyond time.

> It comes this way.
> We cannot explain.

Make of it what you will: disaster rolls
from place to place. No. Disasters roll.
No. They emanate from place. The air

delivers them. Sky and sky. With their
indecipherable missives.

> For every body washing by.
> At the instant the heart
> gives it up—the smoky
> breath. Don't tell me
> it isn't breath.

Tracking the storm from here (his knowing hand)
to here. Cotton-ball pinwheel, how perfectly
symmetrical. Can he explain? Grinning.

> O the weather. O
> story of earth. O
> moved by the moon. O
> man-made currents. O
> circle of influence.

Tracking it. The faces of the dead superimposed
(stops the grinning). Cut to images. Cut to whorl
and the weather woman's beringed hand. O circle
of influence.

We're not talking about it looks like a face,
a profile, an eye. We're saying it is. We're saying
there's more to this. We're saying it's happening.

> What realm is this?
> That? What Other?
> Whence the child comes?

There's the eye tunneling through. Eye.

She's saying *it isn't laid end to end.*
She's saying *one upon the other.*
And the eye. And the heart
which follows the eye.
All the way through.

Invocation

Out of stone
Out of salt-smell
Out of silence and sepulchre
Out of moon-chasing night
Out of dead-of-the-night
Night buoying them up
They come

Out of the mind
Out of dream
Out of reminiscence
Out of figments
Out of gladness
Out of grief
They come

Girls with their earlobes
Boys with their lower lips
Men ravenous
Women of parched thirst
They come

Mothers and eyelashes
Grandfathers and teeth
Fathers with the backs of the neck
Come

Grandmothers and underarms
Daughters and sons aflame
Infants and tongues
They come

O Memory
How you want to cradle them
Drink under the syllables of their lips

How you want to offer them
Your regrets
Tender as fingertips
How you want to punish them
To save them from the deep
O Memory

O Second Sight
They are issuing from corner turns
They are disappearing
They are half-sight
And near-sight
Are out of touch
And into touch

The dead are watching
(See their pupils growing large)
The dead are sleeping
(For they turn their eyes inside)
The dead are swimming
(For the suns are full of distance)
The dead are humming
(For they wander in new sounds)

Pull them into you
Tether your sighs to their hair
Float among them tonight
O Weary Travelers
So they come

Ask them to speak in tongues you cannot know
Listen as if the sounds
Are the bones of prophecy
O Dumbfounded Ones

Show them your birthmarks
Your thin lines
Your braille veins

134

And numb scars
For they have none to trace and lament
Show them

They come in ribboned skirts
They come in linen and earth
They come with nothing to see
They come with everything under the skin
In nakedness
In cloth unwinding
In absence
So they are lovely
So they come

O Cemetery
O Honorary
O Funerary
Night of the Dead
Help them come

The dead are moonstone
The dead are hollow stone
The dead are mist on the bones
In mother-of-pearl

So fear them
And hold them
In the shadow of your ribs
With open palms

Evening of the crossing
Stars of the passing through
Moon-hole beckoning

O Mouth Curve
O Bodies Double
Evening O Evening

Till the worlds converge
On incantation
O Double Life
And Triple Life

The Sumptuous Hunger
Of our wandering
Of this longing
Of our reunion this
Communion-on-earth.

Day of the Dead, 1999

Aleida Rodríguez

Feast of the Epiphany

The infusion of evening is steeping
in the last golden liquid of day,
submerging the backyard in a lavender greenness
where only my neighbor's oranges glow
over the back fence, clinging to the light
and storing it within themselves.
I'm listening to the Fourth Movement of Mahler's Fifth,
holding a tiny glass of amontillado.
Suddenly I remember today
is January 6, the Feast of the Epiphany,
the day three wise men finally
reached the manger to witness the glow
curled within the sleeping child
and felt a sweetness strummed
like a harp within their breast.
Did they also feel a heaviness pulling at them,
the way we feel something materializing
behind the door of our joy,
ready to knock,
maybe not today, so sweet and amber,
but soon?

What the Water Gave Me

for Leonard Sanazaro

The Waterfall

Thunderous locomotion, a roar, rhythmic
clack of freight car, freight car, freight car.
Visible wind on granite face, Saran wrap
hair shaping/reshaping off the forehead.
Let go the head, that cave
from which all bats have flown anyway.
What of the body, then? A black beetle
advances like ancient machinery. The left hand
sweeps it away without curiosity.
So thirsty.

Usurped Corridor

Barely daybreak, a scratching on a post
outside the window. Steller's jay visitation:
blue body bristles, black crest tilts,
hematite eye penetrates sleep.
Unruly cowlick echoes one on the man,
seven and seventy, who stumbles into morning's kitchen—
white robe, swollen eyes—seeking water:
baptismal, disastrous, transformative.

Transparent Bondage

Watery will reshapes history, obliterates evidence,
gets its own way. Riverlike muscle,
a man who has beaten a woman,
carves a course through the brain
to arrive there quicker next time.

Pastoral

Len is sacked out on a recline-o-rock,
taffy-twist of current at his feet.
Near the falls, that mirror force,
he surrenders. His pale body's a gentle landscape.
On the trail he says, "I don't know whether
Arinata Fuccelli is a flower or a soprano."
Log downstream: lost canoe? silver slipper?

Advancing the Plot

Stick washes up at my feet.
I toss it into the frantic whiteness,
praying it forward, down, toward calm.
No such luck. Begins again its antigravity
salmon journey. Again I aim, again
it boomerangs. *Let it go, let it go, go, go,*
the water angel says.

The Invisible Body

I.

In the garden, it's there. Even when you're inside you feel it,
as though it were you standing naked among the weeds,

the tips of the bougainvillea bursting into flame, your nipples
ruffled like the skin of a lake by a breeze.

You worship the invisible body like an old-fashioned lover, from
     afar,
loving the specificity of space between you.

Sometimes at night it stretches out on the empty side
of the bed, stares at you with the length of its invisible surface.

Every contour of your body not filled by you is molded
by the attentiveness of the invisible body, whose breath
     surrounds you.

It's more than prayer it wants—more than language, with its
     conditions.
The invisible body demands you invent new senses to receive it,

new places on your body to marvel at its subtlety,
like the eyes of the deaf percussionist that perceive sound.

II.

The invisible body wants you to become a satellite dish,
tuned to what exists only because your body calls to it.

Like the woman who had her kitchen remodeled to make room
for the microwave she'd entered a contest for. Then won.

III.

When asked whether falling in love was about acquisitiveness,
about the ego, the seventy-five-year-old poet

responded that the ego had nothing to do with it;
it was the need for union with the beloved.

Rumi asks, *Who is it we spend our entire lives loving?*

IV.

How, then, do you measure the invisible body,
which resists commitment but is faithful?

Is it clear who the beloved is, when no clear
body exists that can be measured against a standard?

V.

The invisible body sometimes acquires a body—it's so convincing,
it takes you a while to figure out it's really the invisible body.

Like someone who has been reading your journal,
it has decoded from your petty, daily complaints the open sesame

that slides the stone from the hidden cave's opening
and cleans you out while you sleep, leaving a sarcastic note.

It wants you to know it was doing you a favor, besides,
how else did you think you'd discover the cave's precise location?

When Aphrodite sharpens you, you sacrifice a little of yourself,
willingly, as a knife does, so that you may become better at it.

VI.

This is the point at which the invisible body speaks
in italics, the Ouija board of poetry.

In my mind, says the invisible body, *that time capsule shuttling
through space, I hold, in all the languages of the world,*

*your love, rushed like holographic platters to a table,
steaming into the future long after you've ceased to shine,*

*the silver faces of your beloved bobbing out of the darkness,
the black velvet pillow of your life on which you offer them for
   view.*

VII.

The invisible body is created out of your longing, your longing
compressing invisible molecules together into an absence you
   recognize.

That is the way one blind man sees the world—after the fact,
in photographs he took, once he had passed through it.

Appendix A

A Brief Overview of Cultural and Religious *Mestizaje*

Orlando Ricardo Menes

A concept that embraces as closely as possible the totality of Latin America's complex racial and cultural heritage, *mestizaje* has had an inordinate appeal to the region's writers and intellectuals since the early part of the twentieth century, and U.S. Latinos, as their inheritors, are no exception. Both here and in Latin America, two of the principal theorists and advocates for cultural *mestizaje* have been José Vasconcelos, a Mexican, and Gloria Anzaldúa, a Chicana. In his ground-breaking book *La raza cósmica* (1925), Vasconcelos writes that America, specifically the Spanish-speaking parts, "shall arrive, before any other part of the world, at the creation of a new race fashioned out of the treasures of all the previous ones: the final race, the cosmic race" (*The Cosmic Race: A Bilingual Edition,* trans. Didier T. Jaén. Baltimore and London: Johns Hopkins University Press, 1979, p. 40).

In opposition to the then prevailing view in North America that racial mixing, in particular that of blacks and whites, would result in a debased mongrelization and thus the demise of Western civilization in the New World, for Vasconcelos this mingling of races and cultures from Africa, Europe, Asia, and the native Americas represents a visionary stage of human development. Employing a discourse that integrates aesthetics and anthropology, philosophy and history, he envisions a harmonious integration, a "happy" synthesis, of all "the elements of beauty apportioned today among different races" (p. 31). Indeed, the ideas espoused by Vasconcelos have had a profound and enduring impact across Latin America, not only inspiring artistic movements like *indigenismo* in Mexico and *mulatismo* in the

Hispanic Caribbean, but also constituting the ideological foundation for discourses of national identity that privilege *mestizaje* over those Eurocentric cultural values inherited from Spain.

Without doubt this historic mixing of peoples and cultures occurred as a result of conquest, colonization, and slavery; nonetheless, those proponents of *mestizaje* as a rubric of Latin/Latino identity, while acknowledging the resultant injustices and depredations, emphasize the greater virtues of unity and solidarity. For instance, one only has to visit Mexico City's Plaza de las Tres Culturas to witness this ideology at work. On the site of the last stronghold of the Aztecs and the Spanish cathedral built on those very ruins, a large plaque commemorates the defeat of Cuauhtemoc by Hernán Cortés "as neither a victory nor a defeat, but the painful birth of the mixed race that is Mexico today." The word "birth" is crucial here, for it suggests that *mestizaje* constitutes a kind of phoenix-like resurrection and thus a more accurate description of cultural transformation than clichés like "melting pot" and "salad bowl," so common in English North America.

To my knowledge, Vasconcelos's ideas did not take root in the United States until the appearance of the Chicano movement, specifically with the publication in 1987 of the first edition of Anzaldúa's innovative and compelling *Borderlands/La Frontera: The New Mestiza* (San Francisco: Aunt Lute Books). Writing from the cultural homeland of Aztlán, the mythical birthplace of her Aztec ancestors, that area of ancient Mexico, now the southwestern United States, obtained by the Anglos through conquest, Anzaldúa reinterprets *mestizaje* with new vibrancy and relevance, transforming it into a concept that serves to define her entire existence as a Chicana, indeed, as a Latina. Anzaldúa's language is heteroglossic, reflecting the (pro)fusion of cultural and linguistic modes of her native borderlands: Spanish (standard Castilian, standard Mexican, northern Mexican, Chicano), English (standard, working class, slang), Tex-Mex, and *caló,* that protean tongue with its own hybrid syntax and vocabulary.

Most important, she magnifies Vasconcelos's notion of a utopian hybridity through the twin lenses of feminist and lesbian consciousness. "I will have my voice," she declares, "Indian, Spanish, white [Anglo]. I will have my serpent's tongue—my woman's voice, my sexual voice, my poet's voice. I will overcome the tradition of silence" (p. 81). As a mestiza, she is empowered to bridge dichotomies of race and culture, "continually walk[ing] out of one culture / and into another, / [existing] in all cultures at the same time" (p. 99). As a *lesbiana,* she possesses the ability to become the "supreme crosser of cultures" because of her "strong bonds with the queer" from every part of the world. In poems and prose rich with spirituality (her text a hybrid of critical and creative writing), Anzaldúa's mestiza imagination boldly merges divergent traditions of the sacred (Yoruba, Aztec, Christian, Chinese), in the process constructing a synthetic "divine consciousness" (her term) that is genuinely *cósmica.* For example, one poem that invokes Yemayá, the Afro-Cuban deity of the sea and maternity, to blow down "the wire fence" (p. 25) of injustice concludes with a prayer to the Virgen de Guadalupe.

In fact, Latin/Latino popular Catholicism is especially receptive to incorporating non-Christian elements into a flexible matrix of religious beliefs that might be termed cross-cultural. A first-generation Cuban American, Catholic theologian Roberto S. Goizueta asserts in his seminal text *Caminemos con Jesús: Toward a Hispanic/Latino Theology of Accompaniment* (Maryknoll, NY: Orbis Books, 1995) that Latinos and Latinas "instinctively see the world as a fusion of 'both/and' rather than as a separation of 'either/or' . . . [and are thus] accustomed to living between two perspectives, two interpretive horizons—or, more accurately, three: the indigenous or African, the Spanish, and the North American" (p. 119). One rather obvious and telling example of this tendency is the popularity among Mexican Americans of the votive candle called Las Siete Potencias (The Seven Powers), consisting of the principal deities of the Santería pantheon syncretized as Catholic saints. Certainly this Afro-Cuban religious tradition is outside Mexican culture, yet those *mexicanos* lighting the candle and praying to the image of Christ on the Cross, called Olofi in Santería, are in their own minds actually worshipping the divine within a Christian mind-set.

Another writer who has explored Latino spirituality through the rubric of *mestizaje* is Father Virgilio Elizondo, a Catholic theologian from San Antonio, Texas. Among his contributions to the study of popular Catholicism among people of Mexican origin are many theological and devotional writings on the hybrid origins of Mexico's patron saint, La Virgen de Guadalupe, affectionately known as La Morenita, The Dark One. Father Elizondo writes that la Virgencita "opened the doors for a new trialogue between the Amerindians, herself, and the leaders of the official [Spanish] church. This trialogue eventually brought about the profound synthesis of symbols which is the basis of the mestizo church of Mexico" (*Beyond Borders: Writings of Virgilio Elizondo and Friends,* ed. Timothy Matovina. Maryknoll, NY: Orbis Books, 2000, p. 283). A review of the extensive Guadalupean devotional literature far exceeds the scope of this introduction, but I provide here a brief description of the miracle drawn from the writings of Father Elizondo and Goizueta.

The *Nican Mopohua,* composed in the Nahuatl language of the conquered Aztecs, is the original text that records the miracle of the Virgin's apparition on Mount Tepeyac to Juan Diego, a humble Indian peasant. This mountain was already sacred ground to the indigenous population, one of the four main sacrificial places of the Aztec civilization, and in particular the site where their ancestors had venerated Tonantzin (Mother in Nahuatl), the goddess virgin-mother of the gods. Another cross-cultural element besides place and skin color is the symbolism of flower and song (*floricanto* in Spanish; *xochitl in cuicatl* in Nahuatl) consistent with Aztec theophany.

The revelation begins with Juan Diego being drawn to Mount Tepeyac by the paradisal singing of birds. He then sees a beautiful young peasant girl, La Virgen, whose features are clearly indigenous. She addresses Juan Diego in Nahuatl, his native tongue, ordering him to bring news of her existence to the bishop; however, the Spanish cleric remains unconvinced without some miraculous evidence. After some events take place that confirm for Juan Diego her heavenly identity, this humble man returns to Mount Tepeyac seeking the required proof to take back to the bishop's palace. La Virgen commands him to go up the hill to cut and gather some flowers, which happen to be roses of Castile—aromatic, covered in morning dew, and a physical impossibility in December. He hands La Virgencita the miraculous flowers, and she then wraps them in his *tilma,* a cotton blanket worn over the shoulder. Juan Diego goes once again to the palace, and when the bishop unfolds the garment, not only do the red roses fall to the floor but the image of Our Lady also appears on the *tilma.* Now a believer, the Spaniard orders the construction of a church on Mount Tepeyac, with the blessed *tilma* enclosed in the altar.

As explained by Father Elizondo in his book *La Morenita: Evangelizer of the Americas* (San Antonio, TX: Mexican American Cultural Center, 1980), the image imprinted on Juan Diego's garment contains indigenous symbolism that is worth noting. For example, Our Lady of Guadalupe's dress is pale red, "the color of the spilled-blood of sacrifices . . . the color of Huitzilopochtli-Sun, the god who gives and preserves life . . . himself nourished with the precious liquid of life-blood" (p. 83). The one color that predominates in the mantle is the blue-green of Ometeotl, "mother-father of the gods, the origin of all natural forces and of everything that was" (p. 83). La Virgencita stands upon the moon, the god of night in the Aztec pantheon.

Appendix B

An Introduction to *Ifá* (Santería Divination)

Adrián Castro

Mojúbà Olódùmarè
Oba téere káiyé
Iba she Ólofin ìbà shé Olórun
Alafúnfún oke
Olójo oní ìba réé o
Mojúbà bogbo igba Irúnmolè ojùkòsìn
Bogbo igba Irúnmolè ojùkòtún
Òkànlé-ní-irínwó
Iba shé bogbo Egun idí lé mi, egbé mi
Bogbo Iyalosha ati Babalosha ara órun
Bogbo Oluwo o ní Babaláwo mbe laíye Órun . . .

This is an excerpt of the early sound echoing throughout my house most mornings. Along with the water libation spilled as the above is chanted and the constant jingle of the *òkpèlè*, the divination chain, *yo abro el día*, I begin the day. Indeed many Babaláwo do the same as a matter of course.

Babaláwo, meaning "father of secrets" in Yoruba, are the "high" priests of the Orisha religion. I use "high" in quotations because it is what we are called in English for lack of a better term. Actually Babaláwo are considered *los mayores*, the elder priests and theoretically the most versed in divination, rituals, initiations, healing, and herbal medicine of the tradition. This title of elder is irrespective of the physical age of the priest. Babaláwo are considered eldest because of the arduous training they undergo. Of course, there are priests within the ranks of Babaláwo that due to many years of study and experience are respected as elders among elders.

149

The jingle of the *òkpèlè* and constant mutter or chanting in Lukumí (Yoruba spoken in the diaspora) are familiar sounds to many Cubans. Because the Orisha tradition and specifically Ifá were dispersed through el Caribe y las Américas by way of Cuba and Cubans in the United States, there are many thousands of practitioners from Puerto Rico, Mexico, Venezuela, Santo Domingo, and Panama living in the United States as well as their native countries. Many people arrive at a Babaláwo's house seeking a solution to their dilemmas, seeking an explanation for their predicament. During the incantation the Babaláwo places the divination instruments on the individual's hands, who then takes them to his or her mouth and whispers the reason for divination. The breath contains the word, which contains the plea. The supplicant hands the *òkpèlè* back to the Babaláwo, who continues the incantation, petitioning various Orisha to help this individual, petitioning various ancestors, reciting the great lineage of Babaláwo that came before him. Soon he casts the divination chain.

Òkpèlè is one of the fundamental instruments a Babaláwo employs. Typically it consists of a thin brass or silver chain with eight concave lobes of coconut shell, *òkpèlè* seed (from where the name derives), or silver, or brass, or palm nut spaced more or less equally along the chain. The Babaláwo holds the *òkpèlè* so that four lobes dangle on each side of his hand. And he casts the *òkpèlè* so that the chain falls with four lobes on the right and four on the left. Each lobe has two sides—a concave and a convex. Depending on the configuration of each of the eight lobes, *sale una letra*—an Ódu is revealed. There are 256 possible combinations, or *Ódu,* which are collectively called Ifá. Each of these 256 *Ódu Ifá* contains many stories, histories, proverbs, anecdotes, metaphors, chants, herbal medicine prescriptions, dietary recommendations, rituals, offerings, *trabajos, entre otras cositas.* The full spectrum of human emotions, thoughts, idiosyncrasies, and deeds. Ifá is the basis of the Orisha tradition and the cornerstone of Yoruba/Lukumí culture. Babaláwo specialize in the study of these 256 Ódu. That's why Babaláwo are also called Ifá priests. It is thought that Ifá is the codified knowledge and memory of the Creator, Olódùmarè, as revealed to Orúnmìlà during the creation of the world. Orúnmìlà was the only witness to creation. He was told by Olódùmarè to cover his eyes with his hands but he slyly opened his fingers, thus seeing the creation of human beings, plants, minerals, and animals. He was there when the *ashé*, the life force propelling all living things, was handed by the Creator, when all human beings knelt before Olódùmarè and chose their destiny. Many of his praise poems/*oriki* begin—"*Orúnmìlà elerí ipín ibikeji Olódùmarè*"—"Orúnmìlà witness to creation, second to Olódùmarè." Orúnmìlà, the orisha of knowledge, wisdom, and divination, speaks through this oracle, not in a human voice or in possession of one of his priests, but through Ifá. And it is the word of Orúnmìlà that the Babaláwo interprets and acts on. Orúnmìlà's word is Ifá. When a Babaláwo *abre el día,* opens the day, he begins here, with the word. And it is from here that his actions spring.

Word and Action. For the Babaláwo and adept of Ifá these are two strips woven into a circular cloth. All Babaláwo have a guiding *ódu* that was revealed during his initiation into Ifá. Adepts who undergo a partial initiation into Ifá also receive a guiding *ódu*. An *ódu* that is revealed during initiation is believed to encompass the initiate's past, present, and future life. This advice as spoken by Orúnmìlà functions as a personal guide on how an individual should proceed in his or her life so as to live more harmoniously and with greater fulfillment. Frequently during divination, proverbs and stories related to the guiding *ódu* are narrated and interpreted by Babaláwo, such as which diety/ies the individual should worship, necessary rituals to be performed, possible scenarios and pitfalls to be avoided, dietary and behavior prohibitions, health recommendations, possible vocations, and so on.

But one's guiding *ódu* is not revealed by the casting of the *òkpèlè*. It is done by the other major method of Ifá divination—

Alukín Ifá, the manipulation of *ikín,* or consecrated palm nuts. The Babaláwo holds several *ikín* in one hand and attempts to grab all of the palm nuts with the other hand. Depending on whether one or two *ikín* are left in his hand, he traces one or two lines on the *opón Ifá* (the circular wooden divination tray covered with *iyefá/iyeròsun,* divination powder). Slowly a series of single or double lines is revealed showing an *ódu* on the divination tray. This method of divination is used for initiations and other important events like divination for a community or nation (as is done in Cuba and Miami), naming ceremonies, finding one's patron Orisha—*su "ángel de la guardia,"* or any crucial situation where Orúnmìlà's advice is sought. It is believed that one's *ódu* is inextricably linked to one's past and one's destiny, and will continue to be until one makes the transition to the other world/*Órun.* It is up to the individual to internalize this personal code of knowledge, to bring it to fruition by action, specifically action on the directives of Ifá, with the authorization of Ifá.

This word, Ifá's word, once written on the divination tray, then uttered and vibrated into consciousness, becomes sacred and immutable. The sound of palm nuts conversing (taka-taka-taka-taka), the sound of finger sliding through divination powder, the sound of the *ódu* and related chants together make a symphony that vibrates in the other world. And in the other world *bogbo igba Irúnmolè ojúkòsìn ati bogbo igba Irúnmolé ojúkòtún ati òkànlé-ní-irínwó* smile and send their blessings. *Àború, àboyè, àboshíshe.*

Glossary

Àború, àboyè, àboshíshe: universal greeting to a Babaláwo. Also a blessing said by Babaláwo, meaning "May the sacrifice be offered, may it be done, may it come to pass."

Bogbo igba Irúnmolè ojúkòsìn ati bogbo igba Irúnmolè ojúkòtún ati òkànlé-ní-irínwó: All 200 deities who sit at the right (of the Creator), all 200 deities who sit at the left (of the Creator), and one other (Eshu/Elegba).

Lukumí: "My friend." Generic term referring to the Yoruba slaves brought to Cuba and their descendents/practitioners of the Orisha religions.

Orisha: Yoruba word for deities—Orúnmìlà, Ochún, Changó, Ogún, Obatalá, etc.

Palm nut: the nut/fruit of a particular type of palm tree (*Elaeis Idolatrica*). These nuts are ritually and elaborately consecrated and are believed to be the symbolic representation of Orúnmìlà on earth.

Yoruba: ethnic group residing in West Africa (Nigeria, Benin, Togo) from where many slaves were brought to the Caribbean, the largest numbers into Cuba. Their traditional religion was Orisha.

Permissions

Richard Blanco. "Los Santos of the Living Room" and "Contemplations at the Virgen de la Caridad Cafeteria, Inc." are from *City of a Hundred Fires,* by Richard Blanco, © 1998. Reprinted by permission of the University of Pittsburgh Press. "Relativity" and "Morning on the Shore" are printed by permission of the author.

Adrián Castro. "Cancioncita pa la Ceiba/Song for the Sacred Mother Tree" from *Cantos to Blood & Honey: Poems* (Coffee House Press, 1997). Reprinted by permission of Coffee House Press. "Para la Installation de José Bedia," "The Mysteries Come to the Bridge," and "Forms of Ifá" are printed by permission of the author.

Víctor Hernández Cruz. "The Physics of Ochún" from *American Poetry Since 1970: Up Late,* ed. Andrei Codrescu, © 1993. Reprinted by permission of Four Walls Eight Windows, New York, NY. "La Milagrosa," "Christianity," and "Islam" appear courtesy of Coffee House Press.

Maurice Kilwein Guevara. "A City Prophet Talks to God on the 56C to Hazelwood" and "I Sing on the Day of the Deceased" from *Poems of the River Spirit,* by Maurice Kilwein Guevara, © 1996. Reprinted by permission of the University of Pittsburgh Press. "Cofradía" and "Good Friday" from *Postmortem,* by Maurice Kilwein Guevara, © 1994 The University of Georgia Press. Reprinted by permission of The University of Georgia Press. "The Fifth of November," "Why Given to Be Adopted," and "River Spirits" are printed by permission of the author.

Demetria Martínez. "Psalm" is printed by permission of the author.